To Dear Doris.
Love.
Joy. Christmas 1983

MIRACLES OF HEALING

By the same author:

INTELLIGENT PRAYER

THE TEACHING OF JESUS ON PRAYER

HOW TO PRAY FOR HEALING

COMMONSENSE ABOUT PRAYER

21 STEPS TO POSITIVE PRAYER

MIRACLES OF HEALING

*Studies of the Healing
Miracles in
the New Testament*

by

LEWIS MACLACHLAN

Chaplain to the Guild of Health

EVESHAM

Published by
ARTHUR JAMES LIMITED
THE DRIFT, EVESHAM, WORCS.

First Edition 1968

© Lewis Maclachlan 1968

All rights reserved by the Publishers,
Arthur James Limited of Evesham, Worcs., England

SBN: 85305022 8

ACKNOWLEDGMENT

The Scripture passages which head the chapters have been
taken from the *New English Bible* version by kind permission
of the Oxford and Cambridge University Presses to whom
grateful acknowledgment is made.

MADE AND PRINTED IN GREAT BRITAIN BY PURNELL AND SONS, LTD.
PAULTON (SOMERSET) AND LONDON

INTRODUCTION

by

Alfred Torrie, M.A., M.B., Ch.B., D.P.M., F.B.Ps.S.

AS one of the medical members of the pastoral counselling group which Lewis Maclachlan leads at Edward Wilson House, the Headquarters of the Guild of Health (a centre for the co-operation of minister and doctor in healing), I feel privileged to write a word of introduction to such an inspiring volume. After reading it I was reinforced in my feeble faith that God heals. We live in an age of rapid change. Old terms meaningful to our forebears pass us by. My generation takes reluctantly to the term "ground of our being" for God in Christ. Yet it is more descriptive of the fact that God's healing power exists in every cell of our bodies and has still its ancient Power to heal our need, not as many falsely think, on merit or deserving.

Among the many new conditions requiring healing to-day is drug addiction. The Alcoholics Anonymous movement leads the way here. They insist that the sufferer must wish to be well and say that there is a Power not himself but within him that can heal. Alas! our heroin addicts are so much slaves of the drug that mostly they are afraid to be well.

I welcome the abolition by this author of the distinction between natural and supernatural as if God were still "up there" or "out there". He is, but is also within. Height and depth are the same. William Blake said, "what is without is within."

This is an age of surgical miracles. Spare part surgery, transplants of kidney, liver and heart have already taken place in

5

this country. One feature of the failures is host resistance, the body's rejection of an alien tissue. Skin grafts have always been rejected if from another's skin than our own. To decrease what is called "host" resistance, substances have to be given which also decrease the patient's resistance to infection so that he lives on at risk, like a haemophiliac at danger from cuts and bruises. The word host has two meanings. The Oxford English Dictionary defines it as "a man who lodges and entertains another in his house" so that the patient does not "lodge or entertain" the alien organ. The word is also used as a "sacrifice" often said of Christ and also as the bread consecrated in the Eucharist regarded as the body of Christ sacrificially offered. The words host resistance could also mean resistance to Christ, to the gift of His love and healing freely offered as that "to as many as receive Him He gives them power to become the sons of God" (John i. 12).

As a psychiatrist I regret the suspicion some Christians have of our function. Ferenzi says that it is the "love of the physicians that heals the patient", so that the aims and means are the same as those who feel that Christ is God-filled man, Love-filled. Science has shown that all matter is energy. Christ must have radiated love-energy in a manner that must have healed many not recorded in the Gospels. Nowadays the kinds of disease have changed their emphasis. Infectious disorders are less often seen because of the advances in medical science. The scientists, both medical and non-medical, are instruments and channels of the discovery of the works of nature. De Chardin has helped many to understand the workings of the Creator in His Creation in the material as well as the non-material world.

Society is one of the areas of the world in which healing is required. Social maladjustments are the causes of many stress disorders. As one authority, Querido of Amsterdam, has phrased it, "Stress is apt to become distress." There is a widespread "separation anxiety", because it is felt that Science has slain God. The truth is that God is resurrected under other names, the unifying principle, the integrating factor, the transforming symbol, the Healing Power, and the ground of our being.

Christ's touch has still its ancient power. I want to recant a statement I made on a TV programme on spiritual healing. I said that laying-on-of-hands was a "gimmick". An article by Canon Andrew Glazewski in the London Hospital Gazette of March 1967 has convinced me that there is an unknown physical law behind such healings. As the Canon, who is also a physicist and scientist, says, "Grace never contradicts nature but builds upon it."

At the University I was Secretary of the Student Christian Movement branch. Encounters in the anatomy room with cadavers drove me into the wilderness of doubt and unbelief. Years later the experience of one of my patients being healed by his wife's prayers brought me back into belief again. I am still only a feeble Christian, but firmly believe in the therapeutic community where the team of ministers, nurses, doctors, social workers and others can be channels of Christ's healing power, first having received Him and His forgiveness, for only a forgiven person can forgive. Forgiveness means a Giver. There is no doubt that many outside the Churches are seeking healing of body, mind and spirit, that wholeness that will give them newness of life. This book will certainly aid them in their search for health.

ALFRED TORRIE

London 1968

AUTHOR'S PREFACE

THESE STUDIES in the healing miracles were originally prepared some years ago for the use of Guild of Health prayer groups at Guildford, Surrey, and are now at their suggestion enlarged to make this book. Its simple thesis is that the narratives of healing in the Gospels are entirely credible, and are to be accepted as faithfully observed records of the power of intelligent faith to co-operate with God in situations of human need. The old critical commentaries which relegated the miracles of the New Testament to the category of pious fiction have been outmoded by the commentary of modern experience. Almost every instance of healing in the Gospels has been paralleled not only in the practice of contemporary medicine but also in that of many who are engaged in the Church's ministry of healing.

The fashion of regarding the ancient world as less intelligent than ours and in particular the tendency to profess to worship Jesus Christ as Lord of all and at the same time to impute to Him a theological acumen inferior to our own is not to be encouraged. If we cannot believe today much that the authors of the New Testament believed so much the worse for us. The healing ministry of our Lord has something to say to this century which we cannot afford to ignore. As the Bulletin (No.2) of the Churches' Council of Healing says: "The healing miracles of Christ can so inspire us that as doctors, as patients, or as observers, we can turn bare clinical events into salvation events and disclosures of ourselves and of God."

I am grateful to my distinguished friend, Dr. Alfred Torrie, who has contributed a foreword and has also given me much encouragement and help in the writing of the book, and to Miss M. P. Davies who with great skill and patience prepared the typescript for the press. I would like also to acknowledge the very helpful interest taken in the book by the Publishers who have made some valuable suggestions.

LEWIS MACLACHLAN

Edward Wilson House,
26, Queen Anne Street,
London, W.1.
1968

CONTENTS

		Page
	Introduction by Dr. Alfred Torrie	5
	Author's Preface	9
Chapter		
I.	What is Miracle?	13
II.	The Resurrection	17
III.	Who was Jesus?	22
IV.	Healing by Forgiveness	27
V.	The Touch of Love can Heal	33
VI.	The Withered Arm	40
VII.	The Gerasene Swine	45
VIII.	The Syrian Woman	51
IX.	The Girl in a Coma	57
X.	The Woman who touched Jesus	63
XI.	He makes Everything New	67
XII.	Bartimeus	72
XIII.	Trees Walking	76
XIV.	The Epileptic Boy	80
XV.	Obedience to Law	88
XVI.	A Daughter of Abraham	93
XVII.	The Widow's Son	99
XVIII.	The Ten Lepers	103

CONTENTS

Chapter		Page
XIX.	Simon's Wife's Mother	106
XX.	The Fourth Gospel	110
XXI.	Do You want to be Well?	113
XXII.	One Thing I Know	119
XXIII.	The Strange Case of Lazarus . . .	124
XXIV.	Walking, Leaping and Praising God . .	131

I

WHAT IS MIRACLE?

WHEN ONE is asked *Do you believe in miracles?* the first answer must be another question and one even more difficult to answer, *What do you mean by miracle?* If by a miracle is meant a very astonishing happening, something that takes us by surprise and fills us with wonder, something that we could not have believed possible if we had not actually experienced it, then let us hope that we all believe in miracles. Not to believe in miracle in this meaning of the word would indicate a lack of that sense of reverent awareness of the Spirit which is constantly opening up to us new views of reality. To lose this capacity for awe and for admiration, this response to that which is as yet beyond our understanding, is to lose a very precious faculty and one without which we are unlikely ever to adventure far.

The prevalent attitude to life which seems to say, "I have seen all, I know all, nothing is marvellous or divine to me except my own cleverness", though sometimes worn as a mask, is that of one whose experience must remain narrowly restricted. But this is not what is usually meant by miracle. A miracle in popular speech is an event which can only be explained as supernatural. It is an extraordinary manifestation of divine power. It is something that happens, to the astonishment of all who witness it, for which no natural explanation can be found. If this description of miracle may be accepted for the moment some comments must be made.

(1) The question *What is the difference between miracle and magic?* need not detain us long. Magic is decadent miracle as the fairy stories of folklore are often decadent gospel. *Beauty and the Beast* is a crudely romantic version of the transforming power of forgiving love. The apocryphal tales of our Lord's wizardry (in strong contrast to the restrained records of the Gospels) appeal not to faith but to a primitive credulity and a taste for fiction. Perhaps we ought to amend our definition and say, A miracle is a rational and beneficent act for which no adequate explanation can be found except in the realm of the supernatural.

(2) When we say no explanation can be found we should add *at present* or *in the present state of our knowledge*. It is often said that to one living 100 years ago modern life would have been full of miracles in the sense of inexplicable events. It could be argued that if the New Testament miracles had been witnessed by a modern observer they would not have seemed miraculous.

(3) The miracles, however, are not recorded merely as evidence of our Lord's compassion and deep feeling for the suffering of the people, but as acts of God. They are instances of the kind of thing that God does and are therefore revelations of God's character and purpose. In the Gospels they are a proof of our Lord's authority (Acts x. 38). They are demonstrations of power which has its source not in the natural but in the supernatural. They are not told to excite our wonder so much as to give us assurance that Jesus was inspired and sent by God.

Even if the whole of human experience could be explained in terms of the natural that would not dispose of the supernatural. What is described by one man as a deed of signal providence could be accounted for entirely by natural coincidences. Those who have made up their minds in advance that God never acts (either because He does not exist or for some other reason) will not believe in acts of God, however many they experience. But

14

those who believe in God will expect Him to act, and those who know God as more than a hypothesis will expect Him often to act surprisingly, as anyone who loves us does.

We will not, however, look for God only in the unusual and abnormal. Indeed it is more frequently in the ordinary happenings of life that God is found. To go hunting for God in the uncanny and eerie as though He were a ghost is not a sign of faith so much as of eccentricity. If you cannot believe in the Holy Spirit without the help of glossolalia, or the resurrection without psychic phenomena, you are exhibiting a faith that seems to be in need of stimulants. The supernatural is revealed in the natural, and the natural is never fully understood except as the vehicle and creation of the supernatural, as the material can never be fully explained except as the manifestation of the spiritual. But we must not evade the question of miracles by saying sententiously that all life is miraculous, as indeed it is. The question is, Are there in life signal acts of God which, however they may be explained in terms of human knowledge, demonstrate His active presence?

(4) To describe a miracle as an event which can only be explained supernaturally is not strictly accurate. For even if a natural explanation is forthcoming, if not now at some future time, that is not to say that such an explanation is all that can be said of the event. An event can be both natural and supernatural. To find a natural explanation is not to exclude a supernatural explanation, and to find a supernatural explanation is not to exclude a natural explanation.

A poor widow facing destitution prayed in simple faith that God would provide for her need. The prayer was scarcely said when an envelope containing a £1 note was thrust through her letterbox. Of course there was a natural explanation but nothing could convince the good woman that there was not *also* a supernatural; and indeed she was quite right.

When Peter lay in gaol condemned to death and the Church

prayed for his release, it may have been a very human angel that arranged his escape, and if investigation could be made undoubtedly a quite natural explanation could be found for the whole affair. But this does not rule out the supernatural explanation recorded in the *Act of the Apostles*.

Quite a number of natural explanations have been offered for the conversion of Paul of Tarsus on the road to Damascus, but, though most of them are at least partly credible, they by no means exclude Paul's own explanation of an encounter with the risen Christ.

II

THE RESURRECTION

LIGHT MAY BE SHED on the nature of miracle by a study of the supreme miracle of all, the Resurrection of our Lord. As in the study of other miracles we find here evidence of three kinds. (1) There are the scriptural records which preserve the testimony of the disciples, or at least an early tradition of that testimony. (2) We have the testimony of Church history. As is so often said, the chief evidence for the Resurrection is the rise and expansion of the Church. (3) We have the testimony of our own experience of the living Christ, the testimony of faith.

In examining the Resurrection there are certain questions which, though sometimes taken for granted, must be explicitly asked and answered. For instance we want to know: What was it in Jesus that rose again? Was it His body or His spirit, or both? It was something that caused Him to appear, on certain rare occasions, but His post-Resurrection life was not the same as His life before He died. He did not rise from the sepulchre and walk out into the world to resume His customary social contacts. He did not enter the palace of the High Priest to confront a startled Caiaphas, nor did He suddenly appear before a cowering Pilate in silent vindication of His innocence. He was "made manifest, not to all the people, but unto witnesses chosen before of God." Mary saw Him in the garden, but if there had been other people present would they have seen Him too?

17

How many men were seen walking to Emmaus, two or three? There was *something* of Jesus which became present to such a degree that He became evident to sense. As energy under some conditions takes shape in matter, so the living Spirit of Christ was seen again in bodily appearance.

Such perception is not outside our ordinary experience. In any friend with whom we have a genuine spiritual relationship, what is it about him that we know and cherish? Not his appearance only, however dear that may be; not the clothes he wears, and not the body which is the manifestation of something which is itself invisible. Even the most carnal desire of the body must depend for its satisfaction on the spirit within. Yet this spirit or character or personality – call it what you will – is the real person. A body without the spirit is dead, and a dead body makes no response and is cast out or destroyed, however reverently, because it is nothing in itself. As the gospel says, *It is the spirit* that gives life: the flesh avails nothing (John vi. 63).

It is this invisible entity which is the reality in all of us. All ordinary social and domestic life is a communion of invisible spirits which use their temporary bodies as means of communication. The body is of no permanence or significance except as the temple of the spirit (1 Cor. vi. 19). No matter how much care is selfishly lavished on the body it will soon cease to be. The true value of any man is the character or person which he really is and which wears his body like a garment. It could be said unkindly of some people that their clothes are the most valuable part of them, and there are some, as St. Paul said, who live chiefly in the flesh; but even they, if they live at all, live as invisible personalities or spirits.

Inasmuch as it is our invisible personality that gives us reality and permanence, it is hardly surprising to learn that this real person (or *inward man*) survives death which after all is no more than the dissolution of the material body. In the same way the decay and disappearance of any object could leave an imperishable memory of its significance or symbolic value. Books which have so often been destroyed by governments which feared what they had to say are survived by their purely spiritual, invisible and quite irrepressible content.

It might be argued in the case of some people who seem to be all flesh, and who show little sign of spirit, that when they come to die there will not be much left. Christian faith with its immense charity will not have it so, and asserts that there is something of the spirit (however feeble) in every man. Be that as it may, we can imagine that for some the life after death is not a very impressive existence, whereas for others death seems to be a release into new spiritual energy and power. Are there not those who have died in recent years who in spirit and character and influence remain as a force both in public and private life? They are invisible, as in reality they always were, but they remain a factor in our experience, and perhaps even an influence in world affairs.

If this is true of some of the great spirits of our time, and of all time, how much more must it have been true of Jesus, who was so powerfully alive before His death that it would be quite incredible that after His crucifixion He should make no impact upon those who loved Him. What we should expect, supposing the gospels to have ended with His burial by Joseph in the unused tomb, would be some account of how His living spirit released from the suffering and bondage of the flesh, found fellowship again with the men and women who had loved Him.

But this is just what the gospels do record – indeed they go beyond our expectation and beyond our usual experience of communion with our beloved dead. In doing so, however, they do not go beyond the bounds of credibility. They tell us that some of our Lord's closest friends, and those who had been nearest Him in the covenant of loyalty and affection, actually saw Him and conversed with Him. It was of course of the spirit of Jesus, that is to say the reality of Jesus, that the witnesses of the Resurrection became aware. They were witnesses not merely of the appearances but of that which the appearances signified, and that was that Jesus was living, living as He always had done in the spirit, and now, only as occasion required, in the body.

When they said that He was living they meant not merely that there existed an influence or a feeling or a presence or a reminiscence or a moral power (though all these were doubtless included) but Jesus Himself in His own person. When they said *Jesus is living* they meant *all that ever was essentially Jesus is living*. The Resurrection meant that *that same Jesus* (Acts ii. 36) was as real and available and powerfully present as He had been before His death. It meant more than this, for now He had accomplished that glorious and triumphant death which had made Him both Lord and Christ.

Of what sort the appearances were we have now no means of knowing. Paul put them all together, including that which arrested him on the Damascus road, as though they were all the same (1 Cor. xv. 5–8). In the absence of those who actually experienced them, and described them in such brevity, how can we tell? We are here in the realm of conjecture. One thing is certain: it was not the appearances that caused the Resurrection but the Resurrection that caused the appearances.

Speculation and conjecture are not very helpful. Some very earnest writers claim them as psychic phenomena, such as may be seen at a spiritualist service or in a haunted house. The Gospel records, however, suggest appearances of a far more vivid and authentic nature. To dismiss them as hallucination evades the question of their real significance. Subjective phenomena are different from objective, but not necessarily less real or less worthy of interpretation. To be profoundly moved by a dream is not less a real experience with actual consequences than watching a play or taking part in a conversation. Indeed the dream may turn out to be far more eventful than the experiences we call real. The consequent history of St. Paul's encounter with Jesus on the Damascus road is just as real whether we call that encounter subjective or objective. The sight which I see subjectively may be more meaningful and arresting and transforming than one which I see objectively. Even an objective view is an interpretation of appearances as its significance depends on the viewer's reaction to it.

There are two aspects of life, the Seen and the Unseen, the temporal and the eternal, the natural and the supernatural, the flesh and the spirit. They are not to be set against each other as though they were at war. They are two views of the same activity: neither is fully intelligible without the other. The spirit is manifest in the flesh, the eternal in the temporal. If it were not so, how would we know either? He that hath seen me hath seen the Father (John xiv. 9). God reveals His own nature in that of a Man, and the Man cannot be understood except as the act of God.

This is what we who believe in miracles are trying to say; there is something more in the material than matter; there is something more in the natural than nature. Intriguing as the Resurrection is, it is of God's providence that the unessential evidence has been hid from us. Such questions as, Who rolled the stone? turn the events of the Gospel into a good detective story but contribute nothing of real value to our faith.

The Resurrection does not consist of the empty tomb: it consists in the life of Christ in His Church. Unless His Spirit is alive and active now in the fellowship of all believers our faith, as St. Paul said, is vain (1 Cor. xv. 14).

III

WHO WAS JESUS?

O NE ASPECT of the Resurrection on which much theological study has put too little emphasis is the person of Christ. When we are discussing the Resurrection we must not forget who it is that thus came to life. Jesus was no ordinary man. The very proper insistence of the Church on His divinity must not conceal from us His humanity. Until we have seen Him as a human being we cannot see Him as a divine being. The Gospels reveal Him as a man of immense compassion and love for His fellow creatures, a man of great capacity for friendship, a man of prayer, probably spending as many hours in communion with God as most of us do minutes. He was possessed of spiritual power far beyond that of His contemporaries. If we are right in claiming for the great Hebrew prophets a genius for religion, how much more may this be said of Jesus? He knew more about the unseen and eternal than any other.

Is it so surprising that one who lived so differently from other men should die differently and that His death should be followed by consequences different from those which follow the death of men who live far less intensely and not in nearly such close contact with the sources of spiritual life? If it can be believed that ordinary men and women of feeble spiritual vitality possess some faculty that survives their death is it not reasonable to believe that Jesus, with all His remarkable spiritual power, should live again after His crucifixion? That He failed to do so would be far more incredible than that He did.

It is the fashion now to condemn this mode of reasoning as liberal and humanist, stressing as it does the humanity of our Lord. But this is less than half the truth. The teaching of the Church, based on the testimony of the contemporaries of Jesus, has always been that the divine spirit which has been manifested in many heroic and saintly lives, and is present in some measure in every living person, was in *full* possession of Jesus of Nazareth. For those who believe in God this is a very credible testimony. As others in hours of crisis have been granted a power greater than their own and so have won to heights of achievement which cannot be explained except as examples of divine inspiration given in time of need, so Jesus lived and died in such a manner as to convince those who witnessed His life and death that God was in Him (Col. ii. 9). Those who do not believe in God, or believe in Him only by hearsay, that is to say those who have not observed His presence in life, will not be impressed by this conviction. They will not believe in Resurrection because they do not believe in the life of the Spirit. They have other interpretations of the events on which Christian faith is founded. But those who believe in God and have had experience of His activity must realise that the Resurrection is exactly the sort of thing that God does.

It is hard to believe the Resurrection unless as a part of total Christian experience. God is at work in every situation of need. His creative thought can change not only the bodily condition of His creatures by restoring them to health, but actually transforming their minds and characters in a process of conversion, and even more incredibly altering the whole moral landscape by a completely new layout of circumstances. When we have seen this happening we can hardly be surprised when we hear that Jesus healed the sick, making men and women whole by restoring them to communication with their Maker. What Jesus did all through His public ministry is the same kind of action God the Father took after the crucifixion.

It all depends what we believe about God. Is there a universal spirit to which the spirit in all human beings is akin, a spirit that sustains in being all creation including mankind, responds to human prayers and aspirations and watches over all His children with parental care? Is there a God who so values liberty and righteousness that He will take the hazard of allowing His children to work with Him and share with Him responsibility for the conditions under which they live? Is it as we allow the divine Mind or Thought to dwell within us that we live, and as we keep Him out that we decay and die? If this is the secret of life it is also the secret of the Resurrection. One who was so filled with God could not die for long.

In one sense there are no miracles. It is often said that it needs faith to see a miracle, but on the other hand faith needs no miracles to prove the presence and activity of God (John xx. 29). To faith the healing ministry of our Lord, and His Resurrection from the dead, are not stunning portents that compel us to believe. We who have faith, which after all is only vision to behold the Unseen, see in the Resurrection, as in the miracles of healing, just what one might expect to happen when God is present. It is not the suspension of the natural order but its fulfilment.

As our Lord said on the way to Emmaus, "*Ought* not Christ to have suffered and so entered into glory?" (Luke xxiv. 26). Why should you be overtaken by surprise and grief? This is exactly what you ought to have expected! Or as Peter said later in Jerusalem, when he tried to explain the Resurrection to the people, *It was not possible for death to hold Him* (Acts ii. 24). Of course He lives because it is incredible to anyone who knows Him that He is dead. It is those who have no faith who make the healing ministry of Jesus and even His Resurrection into miracles as though they went beyond all reasonable explanation and needed another miracle to interpret them.

Those who have had experience of the Church's Healing

24

Ministry have no difficulty in understanding the healing miracles of the New Testament. They are instances of what is being done every day within the modern Church. Happily in this century the healing power of Christ has been rediscovered and it is now widely known that "the prayer of faith will heal the sick" (James v. 15).

This healing is not in opposition to that of the medical professions and the health services, but rather in support of and in thankful acknowledgement of medical knowledge and practice as gifts of God. Our Lord used, as occasion required, the homely remedies which were in vogue in His time, so those who pray for the sick to-day are not averse to the use of the best treatments available but thankfully recommend them. These treatments are not however always available nor, when they are, always effective. There are many patients who seem unable to respond to the usual means of healing perhaps because of some deep (or even unconscious) resentment or fear or some emotional disturbance which is itself the part cause of the illness. Until these sicknesses of soul are cured it may be impossible permanently to heal the body.

The relationship of body to spiritual disease is still a subject of research, but many eminent doctors today maintain that some or even all disease is the manifestation in the body of a spiritual condition. We are too much accustomed to think in terms of a tripartite person — body, mind and spirit — but in reality these are only three aspects of the one entity. Who injures the body hurts the mind, and a sick mind can affect the whole morale or spirit of a man. Is not this why our Lord so closely associated the teaching and healing aspects of His ministry when He sent out His disciples to preach the Gospel and to heal the sick? (Luke ix. 2).

A poem is written and out of the invisible mind of the poet makes its appearance as black marks on a sheet of paper. The paper itself is of trifling value. It can be weighed and measured

25

and chemically analysed and reduced to its component elements. Is there nothing more? Nothing for those who cannot read! But for those who can see the Unseen through the Seen there is something here of a significance and worth far in excess of the material, whose only real importance is to have revealed the spiritual. Even if the paper is destroyed, the poem, which is all that has given it real value, will remain a powerful inspiration, though invisible, in the hearts of those who have read it.

When our Lord's body was destroyed all that was real in Him, the part that was eternal, remained in life. And as the spirit had once taken visible shape in His body, and seeing that matter is the manifestation of invisible energy, is it unbelievable that the living spirit could again take to itself a visible existence and be seen and heard by those who were attuned to it, eventually to manifest Himself more permanently in that Body of Christ which is the fellowship of all believers?

Some of the New Testament epistles must have been written within only a few years of the Resurrection. From them we can learn something of what the Resurrection meant to the early Church. It was a signal demonstration of that divine power of which all Christians had evidence in their own experience of fellowship with Christ. The following words could have been written less than twenty years after the Crucifixion: ". . . how vast the resources of His power open to us who trust in him! They are measured by his strength and the might which he exerted in Christ when he raised him from the dead" (Eph. i. 19–20).

IV

HEALING BY FORGIVENESS

"WHEN after some days he returned to Capernaum, the news went round that he was at home; and such a crowd collected that the space in front of the door was not big enough to hold them. And while he was proclaiming the message to them, a man was brought who was paralysed. Four men were carrying him, but because of the crowd they could not get him near. So they opened up the roof over the place where Jesus was, and when they had broken through they lowered the stretcher on which the paralysed man was lying. When Jesus saw their faith, he said to the paralysed man, 'My son, your sins are forgiven.'

"Now there were some lawyers sitting there and they thought to themselves, 'Why does the fellow talk like that? This is blasphemy! Who but God alone can forgive sins?' Jesus knew in his own mind that this was what they were thinking, and said to them: 'Why do you harbour thoughts like these? Is it easier to say to this paralysed man, "Your sins are forgiven", or to say, "Stand up, take your bed, and walk"? But to convince you that the Son of Man has the right on earth to forgive sins – he turned to the paralysed man – 'I say to you, stand up, take your bed, and go home'. And he got up, took his stretcher at once, and went out in full view of them, so that they were astounded and praised God. 'Never before', they said, 'have we seen the like'." Mark ii. 1–12

Also read: Matthew ix. 1–8, Luke v. 17–26

IN THE New Testament instances of healing are events which have been recorded to bear witness to the power of God. They are one way of preaching the Gospel, or of proclaiming the good news that God is reigning and is in control. They do not therefore concern only the people who were healed. At the time they had something to say to the whole community. Today they have something to tell us about the meaning of life.

The evangelists have selected for their purpose a number of the healing acts of our Lord each of rather a different kind, and each conveying a truth of its own. All testify to the will and power of God to heal disease.

Let us take first the well known case of the paralytic who was brought to Jesus on a stretcher carried by four friends. The striking feature of this incident is its apparent identification of healing with forgiveness. That caused some misgiving at the time, and it may raise some questions in our minds today. Yet a close relation between healing and forgiveness can often be observed and is indicated frequently in Scripture. (See Psalm ciii. 3; Jas. v. 15; Isa. liii. 5).

Forgiveness has been given such a large place in the teaching of Jesus and in the doctrine of the Church because it is the power that takes away and abolishes all that separates and estranges men from God and from one another. It is by the forgiveness of God that we are reconciled to His will and brought into harmony and peace with life. The supreme act of forgiveness is seen in the passion and death of Jesus in whom the evangelist saw "the Lamb of God that takes away the sin of the world" (John i. 29), in whom we have redemption by his bloodshed, even the forgiveness of sins (Col. i. 14).

But what is meant by sin? It is not "doing what somebody else thinks wrong". Sin is anything that opposes God and puts our minds out of harmony with Him. It is therefore anything that comes between us and our highest good. Sin is not to be identified with gross evil-doing, for sin is not so much action as a state of the soul. Some sins that society regards as respectable are among the most dangerous, because they insidiously impede the work of God in our lives. All kinds of selfishness and pride and fear and avarice are a menace as well to the body as the soul. Resentment and contempt and anxiety are notorious factors in the production of disease. If they are seldom the sole cause of illness they can retard and sometimes prevent recovery.

Sin is abolished by forgiveness and by nothing else. Many other ways of dealing with sin are constantly being tried but none of them works. Punishment and the acquisition of merit do well enough in fiction, but in real life are unreliable. This is because sin is not merely the breaking of a law or the neglect of duty but an estrangement from God and a failure in love to Him. It is a breakdown in fellowship. St. Paul called it *enmity* against God.

Now if someone has wronged or hurt you, you can wipe out the offence only by forgiveness. That is what the forgiveness of God does. It reconciles us to Him, and restores us to friendship with Him. It so changes us at heart that we become at one with Him.

Our minds are now in unity with the Universal Mind. Our wills, no longer at variance with the divine will, are gladly obedient to the infinite love and wisdom of God. The stupid attitude of hostility towards life, which is just the same as enmity to God (Rom. v. 10), is changed to good will and joy and peace, and so we are released from all crippling inhibitions.

Whether we are seeking health for ourselves or for others we must begin by accepting the forgiveness of God, and the "remission of sins" that gives us freedom from the paralysing effects of a broken communication with the Author of life and health. Have you seen people behaving strangely and awkwardly and stiffly as though they were under some restraint, perhaps of fear or shyness or a sense of guilt? Their bodily movements are cramped by something that has gripped their minds. This could happen quite unconsciously. We could be crippled in body without knowing or remembering the cause.

In such cases no complete recovery could be had except by some authoritative word of forgiveness or release. This is what happened at Capernaum. Suddenly realising the forgiveness of God and all it meant the patient was liberated from his bondage. So to say, *"Thy sins be forgiven thee"* had the same effect as to say, *"Rise, take up thy bed and walk."*[1]

There are some further points of interest in the case of the paralytic. A comparison of the three accounts given by the three evangelists shows where each desires to lay the emphasis. Matthew does not mention the crowd that had gathered within and around the house and so made it hard for sufferers to reach the presence of Jesus. Mark dwells on the ingenuity of the four friends and on the critical attitude of the Scribes who feel that what is going on is improper and dangerous and who have come in a kind of perverted faith that they are sure to find something wrong. Luke uses a curious phrase in verse 17 – *"the power of God was there for Him to heal with."*

There are two more features of this incident that we may pick out for special notice. (1) The paralytic was dependent on the help of friends without which he could not have been healed. The four men who carried him determined to overcome all obstacles to bring this man into the presence of Jesus, who recognised their insistence as an act of faith. Faith can be expressed in action as well as in word, and sometimes better. To confront people with Christ we do not need to be great talkers.

But we cannot do without friends, and our friends cannot do without us. It is a good thing to be independent in so far as that means learning to help ourselves and not to bother other people needlessly. Some people who go in search of healing should learn to help themselves. Those who say in effect, "I'm sorry, I haven't time to pray, won't you good people do it for me?" are deceiving themselves. Nevertheless we all need

---

[1] For a modern instance of the power of forgiveness to heal see Paul Tournier in *A Doctor's Case Book*. English trans. pp. 149–50. S.C.M. Press. Also Dr. Leslie Weatherhead in *Psychology, Religion and Healing*: "The forgiveness of God, in my opinion, is the most powerful therapeutic idea in the world," p. 339 and following pages.

fellowship as we need fresh air, and to try to do without it is to reduce our health.

There is a great deal of good will in the world, an enormous amount of social service, and innumerable agencies for doing things to people for their good. Let us thank God for them all. They are a protest and protection against that widespread indifference to our neighbours which is the real opposite of love. But the only way in which we can really and permanently help our neighbours is to bring them within reach of the source of all good. These four friends did not go on carrying the invalid around. They made up their minds to get the man to the help he needed. But for them the paralytic would not have been healed.

We must never think of ourselves as healers. It is the power of God that is present to heal. But there may be sufferers who will never be healed until by some practical and persistent kindness *we* make it possible.

(2) The theological objections to our Lord's action made by the learned men who were present are not unlike some of the criticisms of the healing movement that are heard today. It is argued that God ought not to heal (except through the usual channels), and that therefore He does not, and that therefore alleged instances of divine healing must be mistaken. A more reverent and scientific theology waits to see what God actually does and then attempts to interpret the facts as best it can.

Who can forgive sins but God only? they asked. They were quite right. All forgiveness is of God, as all sin is offence against God. *We* might as well ask, Who can heal disease but God only? But God uses and requires the service of those who believe in Him. How can anyone know the love of God except through the love of man? If we do not show our love for our brethren how shall we show our love to God? It is in our love for our neighbours, not as sentiment but as service, that God is revealed. We can make the forgiveness of God convincing only by forgiving one another.

Our Lord said that His treatment of the paralytic was a demonstration of the fact that the son of man has the power, or the authority, to forgive sins. *Son of man* in this context is probably not a title for Jesus Himself, but may mean simply *man* or *mankind*. It is the function of humanity to forgive and thus to declare and demonstrate and prove the divine forgiveness. For it is forgiveness alone that can overcome evil.

This is the eternal truth that lies at the heart of the Christian Gospel. Flashes of inspiration have revealed it in the religious literature of many ages, but it is in the death of Jesus on the cross that it is set forth for all the world to see as the wisdom and the power of God (1 Cor. i. 23–24).

The Scribes were right. Every act of true forgiveness is of God, and inspired by God, and may therefore be called an act of God. When we forgive someone who has wronged us it is God who forgives through us. When we withhold forgiveness we are withholding God's forgiveness. This is the solemn truth of Matthew xvi. 19 and xviii. 18 repeated in John xx. 23. There is never any question about God's willingness to forgive, but often the divine forgiveness must be made effective in the forgiveness of man.

A middle-aged man whose employment necessitated his driving a vehicle on the roads began to incur a great many minor accidents. None of these was serious. The man was an experienced driver with a good record of road worthiness. The accidents however became so frequent that investigation was made and a check was kept on the driver's habits. It was found that the accidents occurred almost invariably on days when he had had a quarrel with his wife.

Forgiveness is so important for health in every sense of the word because it is the only way to reconciliation to God and therefore to life. Without forgiveness we cannot be rightly adjusted to our total environment. To be at harmony with life is health and for that forgiveness is essential, both the granting of it to others and sometimes even more the grace to accept it for ourselves.

V

THE TOUCH OF LOVE CAN HEAL

"ONCE he was approached by a leper, who knelt before him begging his help. 'If only you will,' said the man, 'you can cleanse me.' In warm indignation Jesus stretched out his hand, touched him, and said, 'Indeed I will; be clean again.' The leprosy left him immediately, and he was clean. Then he dismissed him with this stern warning: 'Be sure you say nothing to anybody. Go and show yourself to the priest, and make the offering laid down by Moses for your cleansing; that will certify the cure.' But the man went out and made the whole story public; he spread it far and wide, until Jesus could no longer show himself in any town, but stayed outside in the open country. Even so, people kept coming to him from all quarters." Mark i. 40–45

Also read: Matthew viii. 1–4, Luke v. 12–15.

HEALING of any kind always requires faith on the part of someone concerned. In this instance of the healing of the leper, the faith was that of the sufferer himself. He doubtless held the universal belief of his time that disease was of demonic origin, and, knowing that our Lord had power to expel evil spirits, he felt confident that he could be cured by that means. It was easy for him to believe that Jesus had power to heal, but he was not sure that He would be willing.

This leper, in fact, was in exactly the same position that many people are in today. They would not deny that God *can* heal disease, but they are not sure that He is always willing to do so.

Our Lord's answer was an emphatic affirmation of His willingness to heal. *"Of course I will"*, He said, or *"I will indeed"*. Then He put out His hand and touched the man. Those who believe that the Lord Jesus is the perfect revelation of God will see in His response to the leper an indication of the divine will to heal disease.

Sometimes our Lord healed by word alone. In this case there was a special value in His touch. The touch of the hand can often convey something that cannot be expressed in words. Whether it is the formal laying on of hands, or the affectionate gesture of friendship, or the comforting caress of a mother, something of spiritual power can pass from one to another by this silent declaration of concern.[1]

In this instance the touch had peculiar significance, for who would touch a leper! Perhaps no one had touched him for years. Perhaps the most frequent communication that he had with human society was to be told to keep his distance. The man was an outcast. The law made it only too plain to him that he was a social menace. To his wretched physical condition there was added a mental condition that made it even worse. He was one for whom nobody cared, one upon whom the whole community, for the sake of its own preservation, must impose the harshest segregation. (See Lev. xiii. and xiv. and Num. v. 1–14.)

But Jesus was not afraid to touch a leper even though by doing so He was breaking the Law. He made it clear that He regarded the man as a brother and not as the victim of a foul and contagious disease from whom others turned away in horror. Disease might separate the man from his neighbours but it would not separate him from Christ. The touch was an act of love from which others might have shrunk but which the Lord

---

[1] See further, Chapter XVI, p. 95.

saw to be necessary for the healing of one who for so long had been by cruel necessity deprived of any overt affection.

There are many people among us today who are "out of touch". Not only the obvious outcasts and misfits in society but also many more than are recognised as lonely are starved of affection, though often they would not themselves admit it. A doctor observed that one of his patients, an elderly lady, who normally enjoyed good health, had occasional severe illnesses which coincided with periods during which she was estranged from her somewhat temperamental daughter who lived with her. Another woman of more than middle-age suffered a series of slight accidents which became so frequent as to call for psychological investigation. It was found that only when she was hurt did her husband ever touch her tenderly. Adolescent children often need demonstrative love just at an age when consciously they are inclined to scorn it.

Touch is not to be used carelessly. To go around pawing our neighbours will not win their respect. But rightly used it may be a means of grace. It is often said that some people have a special gift of healing touch and this may be so, but we all have the gift in some degree, and dedicated to God it may convey His healing power. Other interesting instances of healing touch await our study in later miracles. Meanwhile let us observe how our Lord used touch in a daring proof of His selfless concern for a sufferer. Would it be true to say that underlying all *permanent* healing there must be love?

Some of our most thoughtful physicians tell us that one important factor in disease, which deserves the attention of the community, is the sense of being left out and not wanted. Much eccentric and even some criminal behaviour is an over-compensation for a feeling, which may be only partly conscious, of being neglected. Not only small children but also adolescents, and men and women in much later life, can suffer in body through the habitual sense of being unwanted by society. But why should they? Those of us whose own social position is established and secure may in fact take the view that people who feel like this are over-sensitive and must be sick in mind to begin with or they could never take such a stupid attitude to society. Who do they think they are to command the attention of their neighbours?

We must appreciate the fact that people who want recognition by their neighbours and demand their rights are moved by a quite normal and natural desire, though it is one that they are unlikely to understand themselves. We all have a deep and largely unconscious craving for a right relationship to the community in which we live. We are made to love and to be loved, and this demand of love is more important to us than perhaps any other urge of our human nature. There is no need to be sentimental over it. Attribute it if you like to the herd instinct, or more correctly to the wisdom of the Creator who made us with a passion for fellowship that cannot be denied without suffering, but however it is to be explained we must recognise that when it remains dissatisfied it becomes a frequent cause of sickness.

A very attractive adolescent girl developed an apparently uncontrollable habit of petty theft. The articles she stole were usually of little value and she made no effort to conceal her delinquencies. When she appeared in Court her extraordinary good looks won her the special interest and consideration of police and magistrates alike. Once she confided in her probation officer, "The only time people take any notice of a girl like me is when she breaks the law. Sure I have friends of my own class — they're all scum! I want to be in touch with nice people."

The desire to be noticed and touched may even exceed the desire for affection. It can be a factor in predisposition to illness as well as to mischief.

There is another way of looking at this incident of the healing

of the leper. In verse 40 the words with which the leper ad-
dresses Jesus may be a conventional courtesy such as was used
by patients in flattering approach to eminent physicians. They
would say in effect: "Of course I know that no disease can
withstand your skill. It is only a matter of my winning your
favour." Epictetus uses almost identical words in satirising the
silly subservience of polite society to the popular healers of the
day. So it may be that the leper was approaching Jesus with the
sort of phrase that would have been considered appropriate in
seeking the help of a famous consultant.

The response of our Lord to the leper's appeal is also
variously interpreted. An early reading of verse 41 has *moved
with indignation* instead of *moved with compassion*, and this is
the text approved by the translators of the *New English Bible*.
Why Jesus should have been angry is not quite clear at first
sight, and perhaps it is for that very reason that an early copyist
changed "anger" to "compassion", considering that more reverent and better sense. When the evangelist attributes anger to our
Lord he means deep emotion (as we shall see in Mark iii. 5).

Perhaps the original record bore witness to the fact that the
sight of this horrible plague moved Jesus not only to pity for
the sufferer, but also to a kind of indignation as of one who
would protest against all disease. It is as if our Lord had said in
effect: "This is not right! This foul disease calls not only for
sympathy for its victims, but also for abolition in the name of
God! You ask me if I am willing to heal you. What do you take
me for? Do you suppose that I would hesitate if I had the
power to cleanse humanity of this for ever? Do you suggest that
I could tolerate this loathsome sickness? Is that the sort of man
you take me to be? Or do you think that God in Heaven has
ordained that the human beings He has made should become a
prey to such hideous afflictions? No! As God reigns this calls
for expulsion!"[1]

[1] See *The Faith that Rebels* by Professor D. S. Cairns, S.C.M.

Is it possible that we have become too complacent about disease instead of being moved by it to a Christlike hostility? We hear much of patients learning to "live with" their diseases. Are we all as a community too much inclined to be reconciled to sickness? It can provide such opportunities for charitable employment. Many invalids have got so used to their infirmity that they could hardly do without it. Such was the lady of whom her doctor said "She *could* be cured, but the shock would probably kill her." A chronic weakness can be like a good handicap in the game of life and an excellent excuse for failure to achieve ambition. For Jesus disease was an enemy, an outrage against the blessed will of God. It was not to be tolerated. It was a flagrant violation against God's holy will and had no place whatever in His Kingdom.

As soon as He had healed him our Lord drove the man away (it is the same word that is used in v. 12) with two emphatic instructions, (1) He was to go at once to the priest, as the law required, to have his healing certified. There should be no comma after "commanded" in the A.V. The man is not to testify to the healing of Christ, he is only to satisfy the authorities that he is no longer a leper. (2) On the other hand he is not to say anything about the healing to anyone. This may have been to avoid publicity, as the evangelist thinks, though public registration of the cure seems hardly compatible with an attempt to hush the matter up. When we receive divine healing there are good psychological reasons for not talking about it too soon. Reminiscence of past troubles, no matter with what good intention, may bring about a recurrence of them. It is better to remain quietly thankful, dwelling in our thought not on the disease that has gone but on the health that has come, and not upon ourselves but upon our Saviour. Only when the healing or other recovery has become fully established can we discuss it with safety. The word translated "strictly charged" in Mark i. 43 suggests an emphatic command. It has been supposed that

38

the incident took place in a house and that therefore the leper
had transgressed the law and caused embarrassment to Jesus
by coming indoors. But there is nothing in the text to suggest
such unlikely circumstances.[1]

[1] See C. E. B. Cranfield, *St. Mark*, Cambridge U.P., p. 94 (paperbacked).

VI

THE WITHERED ARM

"ON another occasion when he went to synagogue, there was a man in the congregation who had a withered arm; and they were watching to see whether Jesus would cure him on the Sabbath, so that they could bring a charge against him. He said to the man with the withered arm, 'Come and stand out here.' Then he turned to them: 'Is it permitted to do good or to do evil on the Sabbath, to save life or to kill?' They had nothing to say; and, looking round at them with anger and sorrow at their obstinate stupidity, he said to the man, 'Stretch out your arm.' He stretched it out and his arm was restored. But the Pharisees on leaving the synagogue, began plotting against him with the partisans of Herod to see how they could make away with him." Mark iii. 1–6.

Also read: Matthew xii. 9–14, Luke vi. 6–11, xiv. 1–6.

COULD ANYONE be so perverse as to oppose the healing of disease? Strangely enough some good people are opposed to healing unless it is done in the way that they think right. In this incident we see how our Lord was being watched suspiciously by those who were trying to collect evidence for His prosecution. There was a man in the synagogue whose arm was paralysed, and the opponents of Jesus were sure that this man would so appeal to His compassion that He would heal him on the spot. They were not concerned for the sufferer; they were only using him as a trap in which to catch their prey. It was this unfeeling conduct that roused our Lord to indignation. He was "grieved by the hardness of their hearts".

The tragedy of this is that the Pharisees, who seem to have led the opposition against Jesus, were perhaps the best part of the nation. They maintained a high standard of religion. Yet they were scared by the power of Jesus, fearing that it could upset good customs and endanger tradition. They were quite right in valuing the Sabbath as a religious discipline and a social asset. But it was recognised that the ordinarily binding provisions of the law must be set aside on grounds of mercy. Even on the Sabbath it was permitted to go to the rescue of a dumb animal in distress or danger.

According to Matthew our Lord pleaded with them that since that was so, as everyone knew, then surely it must be right to deliver a man from his infirmity even on the Sabbath. There was however a difference between the man who had the paralysed arm and an animal who had stumbled into a pit. The man could have waited till the next day without suffering more than a brief continuance of his infirmity, whereas the animal might have been in pain and in danger of its life. But Jesus insisted that the same principle of compassion which allowed exceptions to the law in the case of perishing livestock (Exod. xxiii. 5: Deut. xxii. 4) applied to the rescue of any victim of disease. This passage shows that our Lord regarded illness as so contrary to the will and law of God that it must be treated as an evil to be immediately attacked and overcome. The idea that disease might sometimes be the will of God or made to serve His purposes seems never to have occurred to Him.

Matthew uses a version of the controversy between Jesus and the Pharisees which Luke inserts at xiv. 3–5 in recording the healing of the man with dropsy. The actual healing seems to be regarded here as almost incidental. It was the normal procedure whenever the Lord was confronted by disease. What really impressed and astonished the evangelists was the opposition to the Gospel on the part of the very people who ought to have welcomed it most.

There are good people today who are opposed to healing unless it is done in accordance with their own teaching. The Christian Scientists, who have made such a world-wide witness to the healing power of the spirit, are opposed to the work of the medical profession. Many dedicated doctors regard all healing that is not under medical control as dangerous. When we exalt our own idea of what is right, our own conception of the Law above the needs of those who suffer, we may expect to see the Lord looking round in anger.

Anger, however, may not be the best translation. Deep feeling, rather than indignation, is what is meant by Mark x. 14. That our Lord was frequently seized by fits of righteous indignation is very unlikely, but still more unlikely is it that He walked through life in the serene tranquillity of one who was impervious to any real feeling. Was He not on all points tried as we are and very much more severely than most? (Heb. iv. 15.) He was confronted daily by a world that moved Him deeply and by appeals and revulsions that went to His heart. This is what the Gospel calls anger, more akin to the moving speech of the inspired preacher or great statesman than to the outburst of fiery opposition that sometimes is only a substitute for strong and effective action.

The instantaneous healing of the man in the synagogue has been paralleled by modern psychiatry. In his contribution to *Pyschology and the Church*, published by Macmillan in 1925, Dr. J. A. Hadfield said "Practically all the healing miracles of the New Testament have been reproduced in shellshock hospitals over and over again." Modern instances of healing by psychotherapy or other treatment are certain proof of what we already knew, that there is a power of the Spirit to heal which may be manifested in a large variety of ways. All healing is of God, who often uses many human agencies to accomplish His purposes, and sometimes none at all. To quote Hadfield again (p. 255), "All forms of cure are, therefore, alike in this, that they merely liberate certain curative forces, call them the *vis naturae medicatrix*, instinctive emotional forces, or spiritual forces, which are alone the agents of healing. No physician, surgeon, psychotherapist, or spiritual healer ever healed anyone; they only put the patient in the way of healing."

Nearly fifty years ago Dr. Creighton Miller told of a soldier whose right arm was paralysed and entirely useless. When all available treatment had failed to cure him the day came when the doctor said "Well, we'll just have to discharge you; the papers are all ready. I will sign them if you will pass them over to me." The man seized the papers and handed them to the doctor with the hand that had been paralysed!

Does that make this incident more credible? One commentator naïvely says, The Healing Miracles of the New Testament are no longer an offence to faith since modern medicine has shown them to be quite possible.

That sounds as though we believed in Christ by kind permission of the natural scientists, which would be just as absurd as for a man to say, "I'm so thankful I can now love my wife and children because the lawyers say there's no objection." Belief in God is derived not from any external authority but from our personal experience of His grace. But the testimony of modern science may well be taken as a warning to us not to reject as improbable or untrue everything that we cannot yet explain on scientific grounds. It seems reasonable to suppose that Jesus was so far in advance of His time that the world will need a few more centuries to catch up with Him!

A Free Church minister in England suffered from an infirmity of the spine which notwithstanding regular treatment grew worse until he found difficulty in conducting services in his church. At last he had to avail himself of the arrangements for sick leave which his religious denomination generously provided, but when he had been absent from duty for some months it became obvious to all that something would have to be done and the Church decided to obtain the advice of one of the best consultants in the country. The verdict was that there was no hope of recovery or even of a temporary improvement in the minister's condition. The disease would gradually spread until the patient would be confined to an invalid chair.

Reluctantly the minister was asked to resign his charge and arrangements were made for his retirement. This development, though it might have been foreseen, came to the minister as a challenge to his Christian faith, and he now sought the healing power of Christ through prayer. He entered a home of healing where meditative prayer was taught and practised and within a few months underwent a remarkable recovery. Not only was he able to walk but he also resumed his duties as a minister and was able to undertake the arduous work of a country parish, walking long distances to visit his scattered people in a farming community. When he finally reached retiring age he was in excellent health and continued to lead an active life in the city.

It is often said that all healing is of God. This is profoundly true, but the power of God is put into operation by the faith and co-operation of man. It is by the realisation of this omni-present power, that is by giving our thoughts to serve the thought of God, that we bring it into evidence. Most of us are not sufficiently aware of God to be very effective conductors of His power. But Jesus not only demanded of His disciples that high degree of sensitivity to divine action, which He called *faith*, but so exercised it Himself as to make manifest to all the latent healing power of the Spirit.

VII

THE GERASENE SWINE

"So they came to the other side of the lake, into the country of
the Gerasenes. As he stepped ashore, a man possessed by an unclean
spirit came up to him from among the tombs where he had his dwelling.
He could no longer be controlled; even chains were useless; he had
often been fettered and chained up, but he had snapped his chains
and broken the fetters. No one was strong enough to master him.
And so, unceasingly, night and day, he would cry aloud among the
tombs and on the hill-sides and cut himself with stones. When he
saw Jesus in the distance, he ran and flung himself down before him,
shouting loudly, 'What do you want with me, Jesus, son of the Most
High God? In God's name, do not torment me.' (For Jesus was
already saying to him, 'Out, unclean spirit, come out of this man!)
Jesus asked him, 'What is your name?' 'My name is Legion,' he
said, 'there are so many of us.' And he begged hard that Jesus
would not send them out of the country.

"Now there happened to be a large herd of pigs feeding on the
hill-side, and the spirits begged him, 'Send us among the pigs and
let us go into them.' He gave them leave; and the unclean spirits
came out and went into the pigs; and the herd, of about two thousand
rushed over the edge into the lake and were drowned.

"The men in charge of them took to their heels and carried the
news to the town and country-side; and the people came out to see
what had happened. They came to Jesus and saw the madman who
had been possessed by the legion of devils, sitting there clothed and
in his right mind; and they were afraid. The spectators told them
how the madman had been cured and what had happened to the pigs.
Then they begged Jesus to leave the district.

"As he was stepping into the boat, the man who had been possessed begged to go with him. Jesus would not allow it, but said to him, 'Go home to your own folk and tell them what the Lord in his mercy has done for you.' The man went off and spread the news in the Ten Towns of all that Jesus had done for him; and they were all amazed." Mark v. 1–20.

Also read: Matthew viii. 28–34, Luke viii. 26–39.

THE GOSPEL NARRATIVE makes it plain that the healing ministry of our Lord met with suspicion and hostility. This would be almost incredible but for the fact that it is still the same today. For this strange opposition to the healing work of Christ (we might find an analogy to it in the widespread antagonism to work for world peace) there are various motives. In this incident we see that the healing of a mental sufferer led to some disturbing consequences. We must note that the contemporaries of Jesus did not dispute the evident fact that He exercised a wonderful healing power. But, they said, there are other values even more precious than health and these must be protected. Exactly the same thing is said today.

All sickness was attributed to possession by evil spirits, and mental derangement seemed obviously to be caused by some alien spirit or demonic being taking possession of the afflicted person. Whether we regard this belief as entirely primitive and unscientific, or as one way of trying to express a real truth, the fact to be noted is that it was universally held in the ancient world and by some very intelligent and devout people. Not only the New Testament but classical literature also has many allusions to this generally accepted theory of disease and its cure.[1]

Did our Lord share this belief of His time, or did He graciously accommodate Himself to the popular understanding? In some of the other miracles He seems to have made no use of

[1]Read for instance *The Mind of Jesus* by Dr. William Barclay, Chapter 9. S.C.M.

exorcism nor to have made any concession to the theory of demon possession. But in this case, so strong was the belief, both of the invalid himself and of the whole community, that he was the victim of unclean spirits, that perhaps this was the only way by which the man could be restored to health.

It was part of the popular belief that for successful exorcism the name of the possessed person must be known and used (cf. Gen. xxxii. 29).

Several cases of obsession in recent years could be recalled in which Christian ministers have used an act of exorcism to give relief to patients who so intensely believed themselves to be possessed by evil spirits that other treatments had proved unavailing. This kind of prayer was used not so much because the ministers who did so believed in demonic possession but because the patients did, and seems to be justified by its results.

Instances of healing by the spoken word are not infrequent. A young man who believed himself to be possessed by an evil spirit was tormented by irrational fears which attacked him with special vehemence during the night. Physically and mentally exhausted he appealed for help to the Church where a simple service of prayer in the presence of a small group of believing people was held. After the reading of scripture, and a brief explanation of what was being done, prayer for peace of mind and perfect reconciliation to God was offered, ending with the words of exorcism from the Gospel, "In the name of the Lord Jesus Christ *depart and come out of him and enter no more into him.*" A time of meditative prayer followed after which the young man went away evidently much relieved. After several years there had been no relapse and the young man was last reported to be in excellent health of mind and body.

In this Gospel record of healing, however, the sick man is a dangerous maniac, an object of fear to the whole community. His unnatural physical strength had defied efforts to put him under restraint. Short of taking his life there was nothing to be done but to leave him to inhabit the hillside tombs, which were the reputed haunt of evil spirits, in the hope that he would keep out of sight and make as little trouble as possible.

Such a man was a challenge to the Gospel and a challenge which Jesus was ready to meet. With the whole populace staring at him in horror as a menace to their peace and safety was it any wonder that the deranged man had tendencies to violence? Insane persons often exercise an uncanny gift of perception, perhaps because their unconscious faculties are nearer the surface of the mind and unimpeded by conventional behaviour. Anyhow this man recognised in Jesus, not the Messiah but a person of exceptional power, and realised there was that in Him which was a danger to something in himself.

The conversation between our Lord and this maniac was probably much longer than the brief account of it given in the Gospel narrative. We can imagine that Jesus won the man's confidence and assured him that he could lose his sickness, and the devils that caused it, without suffering any real harm. It is curious how some patients need reassurance as to the desirability of health.

Objection has been made to this act of healing on humanitarian grounds. How could Jesus inflict death on so many innocent creatures? This tender feeling for the sufferings of swine is touching, and we trust that those who express it are themselves vegetarians. People who kill many more pigs than this every day – either personally or by proxy – cannot very sincerely find a moral fault in the destruction of even such a large number as two thousand to save a man's sanity. But it is not necessary to suppose that Jesus deliberately accomplished the destruction of the herd. According to the communal belief the outcast spirits must have somewhere to go and the suggestion that they should take possession of a nearby herd of pigs was natural. Mark says that our Lord gave them leave to do so, thus humouring the deranged man, who needed some emphatic assurance that his unclean spirits had left him. What followed can hardly have been part of our Lord's purpose. Some suppose that the herd took fright and that the people present, believing as they did in demonic possession, attributed their stampede to the spirits. Perhaps we have here an instructive instance of the power of the communal mind both for evil and for good.

It is curious to observe that so many of our Lord's acts of healing provoked opposition. In this case there seemed to be an unnatural desire on the part of the local community that He should go and leave them in peace. Whether He was actually to blame for the loss of the pigs or not, they could see that He was a man possessed of unusual powers. On the whole it would be safer not to have Him around. Within their own narrow limits they were quite right: no study of the New Testament has ever suggested that Jesus was an easy man to live with. To get something one does not have, one has often to give up something one has (Matthew xiii. 44–46). All that Christ could have given those people was lost to them because they would not part with what they had.

The healing of the mentally sick has advanced slowly through the centuries and is still far from the standard set us by Christ. Imprisonment in varying degrees of comfort, with or without sedation, has been the best that most communities could do until quite recent times. Psychiatry has brought the possibility of treatment to many sufferers whose cases even at the beginning of the century, would in most countries have been hopeless. More recently the therapeutic value of persistent friendship and caring, and the reorganisation of mental hospitals so as to give more occupation as well as more liberty to patients has been an important advance.

These improvements in the treatment of mental invalids can be traced back to the example of our Lord who with the courage of a great love made friends with one who felt himself isolated and unwanted by all. The whole community had made an enemy of him and it was little wonder therefore that he made enemies of all who came near him. Restraint and incarceration, while they appear necessary for the protection of the public, seldom fail to do more harm than good to the patient. Jesus, with His divine care for the human person, and His immense faith in God, made contact with that in the sufferer which was not dangerous or insane but was akin to his Maker and a potential child of God. The result was a change of character even more miraculous than the healing of physical disease.

VIII

THE SYRIAN WOMAN

"THEN he left that place and went away into the territory of Tyre. He found a house to stay in, and he would have liked to remain unrecognized, but this was impossible. Almost at once a woman whose young daughter was possessed by an unclean spirit heard of him, came in, and fell at his feet. (She was a Gentile, a Phoenician of Syria by nationality.) She begged him to drive the spirit out of her daughter. He said to her, 'Let the children be satisfied first; it is not fair to take the children's bread and throw it to the dogs.' 'Sir,' she answered, 'even the dogs under the table eat the children's scraps.' He said to her, 'For saying that, you may go home content: the unclean spirit has gone out of your daughter.' And when she returned home, she found the child lying in bed; the spirit had left her."
Mark vii. 24–30.

Also read: Matthew xv. 21–28.

THIS IS an instance of healing at a distance. Matthew has modified what is probably the original narrative in Mark, emphasizing our Lord's reluctance to extend His healing ministry beyond the boundaries of orthodox belief. This is in accordance with the customary tendency of the first Gospel to present Jesus as the Messiah sent primarily, if not exclusively, to God's chosen people.[1] Any exception to this rule, he implies, must have been justified by unusual circumstances, and our Lord, he believes, could have been persuaded only by special considerations to break His rule as laid down in Chapter x. 5–6.

[1]But cf. Matthew viii. 5–13, another case of the healing of a Gentile.

He even hesitates to record that our Lord had found a lodging in a heathen house and makes the suppliant woman come out of her own country of Syro-Phoenicia to find Him walking with His disciples, presumably somewhere in Northern Galilee.

Mark simply records that while Jesus had sought relief from the pressure of publicity, and perhaps safety from the jurisdiction of Herod, He was too well known to escape attention. The woman, though not of Jewish faith, had heard of Him and sought Him out, moved by anxiety for her daughter. She was probably a person of social standing as well as of intelligence. To say that her daughter was possessed by an evil spirit may mean no more than that she was seriously ill, as all diseases were ascribed to demonic possession.

The question raised by the evangelists is one which is still with us. Can non-believers receive divine healing? Too prompt an affirmative answer may indicate failure to perceive the real question. What would your response be to someone who said, "I have no belief in God, but my child is desperately ill and I want you to heal her as I know you can." A man who came to ask for prayer declared, "I'm a member of the Church but I have been a practical atheist for years. I've just been told at the hospital that I'm dying and they can do nothing for me. But can't *you* do something?" What would you say to such a request? What would our Lord have said? Is it surprising that He had some questions to put to this woman before He could help her?

It was unlikely that she had an orthodox faith in God. She was one of those who are driven by need to seek help for a loved one. What kind of faith had she? Perhaps no more than faith in a Man of whom she had heard as a renowned healer. It was the quality of her faith that Jesus had to test. After a talk with her He was satisfied that the woman had enough belief in Him, and in the power of God through whom He claimed to work (John xiv. 10), to put that power into operation.

What our Lord said to this woman raises some questions for

those who practise intercession for the sick. Churches and prayer groups regularly receive requests for prayer on behalf of people at a distance. Some of these perhaps are given too unthinking a response, and a too unconditional encouragement to expect recovery. Some organisations which deal with large numbers of clients are content to issue circular letters assuring applicants that their requests have been accepted and that prayer is being confidently made for the healing of the person concerned. This procedure seems to go beyond the practice of some of the earlier leaders in the Christian ministry of healing and to ignore the caution exercised by our Lord in this and some other instances.

There is no question of discrimination between the deserving and the undeserving (a distinction which would be foreign to the Gospel) or between the orthodox and the unorthodox. The question is, must there be some degree of faith in the person who makes the request or in the person for whom the request is made, or perhaps in both? The answer could be that unless some faith were present the request would not be made. But why then did Jesus press His questions on the mother of whose anxiety for her daughter He could have had no doubt? Because for healing, genuine concern is not enough, nor is a credulous disposition to believe that there *may* be something in religion after all. People who do not usually pray show very clearly that, whatever their profession may be, they do not believe in prayer and therefore have a very nebulous belief in God.

Do we need to give more instruction in prayer to those who come to ask our help in intercession? If their minds are filled with anxiety and depression and the conviction has gripped them that the worst is sure to happen, it may be hard for our prayers to break through such resistance. Victims of fear claim our deep compassion, and there must never be the slightest reproach or impatience towards those who do not believe as we do. Nevertheless it is hard to help those who, over many years perhaps, have succumbed to the habit of negative feeling. Before we can obtain for them the aid they need it may be necessary for them to undergo that kind of repentance or change of mentality which consists in believing the good news.

Some prayer groups issue to those who request their help a letter or leaflet stating briefly the principles of Christian prayer. Faith is not the same as credulity, still less is it a good-natured disposition to agree with everything that is said. It is our fundamental belief in the nature and purpose of life. Our faith is our belief in God, and that means what we believe about the ultimate power in life and the relation of the material to the spiritual. To the man who says, perhaps in fear and desperation, "I don't believe but please pray for me", the answer in the name of Christ cannot be "Go away – you are outside the scope of God's healing power." But it might have to be something like this: Prayer is neither sentimental nor magical; it is obedience to divine law. God's will is to heal the body as it is to save the soul, but to accomplish His purpose He uses the faculties that He has created in man. If these faculties are not put at His disposal, as they are in prayer, but used rather to hinder and thwart the divine purpose, then God's will may remain unfulfilled. The all-holy God, our heavenly Father, is not one whom we have to induce to act in our favour. He is ceaselessly active to heal, as to save. The question is, can He induce us to trust Him sufficiently to allow Him to use our thoughts and desires to put His essentially good will into action?

We cannot believe that Jesus made difficulties for the Syrian, but He wished her to face reality. There exists in life a tremendous power for good, a power of the spirit which works through the minds and beliefs and the prayers and desires of those who believe in it. Those who, whether from ignorance or enmity, refuse to co-operate with the divine spirit, hinder and perhaps sometimes altogether prevent the working out of God's purpose. Was our Lord saying in effect: We who believe in God, and who trust His loving power to heal, so indeed become the instruments and objects of His loving power, but how can we extend the good news of God to those who do not share our faith, who perhaps have a quite different belief in God, if any? If you are clinging to a pagan faith, if you believe that God wills or tolerates disease, or that He is reluctant to do for mankind what all decent parents would do if they could for their children, how can you expect to experience His healing power? Is it of no consequence after all whether we have a true faith in God or not? Can you believe in some monster of your own imagination instead of in the living true God, and yet expect God, as He has revealed Himself to faith, to be as active in you and for you as if you had always worshipped Him? Does it make *no* difference whether or not we have a true faith or a false? The answer is, Yes, indeed, it makes all the difference and, thank God, there are those who do hold a practical faith and witness to it.

But true believers exist not for themselves alone but are by their very nature a blessing to the whole community. The Church exists not for its own salvation but for the salvation of the world. Those who are called to pray, pray not for themselves only but for all. There is always an overspill of God's goodness from the believer to the unbeliever, from the household of faith to its neighbours. Wherever there is a feast, there must be crumbs for the comfort of many whose right to be there must be questioned though not their need.

The important characteristic of the Syrian Woman was her persistent trust. She was an example of that importunity which our Lord had praised in some of His parables (Luke xi. 8, xviii. 1-8). If as the narrative suggests Jesus made demands on her, they were demands which she was determined to satisfy. She was sure that Jesus could help her and she was not going away without His help. How different her attitude was from that of much feeble prayer which seems to say

55

apologetically, "I'm not sure whether you can, Lord, and I don't suppose you will." This woman trusted Jesus – she was sure He both could and would come to her aid. It was only a question of putting her request to Him with enough persistence. She did not know that the hindrances the Lord put up were all part of His device to draw out her faith and to deepen within her the trust that will not accept refusal.

We can imagine that the conversation as recorded is very much condensed. What our Lord said about throwing the children's food to dogs was probably not so harsh as it sounds in translation. He used a diminutive as though to say, "It can't be right to give the children's food to their pets." The woman's witty rejoinder convinced Jesus that she understood, and He hesitated no longer but sent her away with the assurance that she would find her daughter healed. She took his word for it and was not disappointed.

The whole story shows that there is a power in life, whether we call it natural or supernatural does not matter, which can be put into operation by our trust in it. This healing power of God does not depend for its efficacy on physical proximity or the touch of hands, however helpful these may be when available. The grace of God can be communicated in "absent treatment" just as effectively as by actual ministration.

IX

THE GIRL IN A COMA

"As soon as Jesus returned by boat to the other shore, a great crowd once more gathered round him. While he was by the lakeside, the president of one of the synagogues came up, Jairus by name, and, when he saw him, threw himself down at his feet and pleaded with him.

"'My little daughter,' he said, 'is at death's door. I beg you to come and lay your hands on her to cure her and save her life.' So Jesus went with him, accompanied by a great crowd which pressed upon him. . . . While he was still speaking, a message came from the president's house, 'Your daughter is dead, why trouble the Rabbi further?' But Jesus, overhearing the message as it was delivered, said to the president of the synagogue, 'Do not be afraid; only have faith.' After this he allowed no one to accompany him except Peter and James and James's brother John. They came to the president's house, where he found a great commotion, with loud crying and wailing. So he went in and said to them, 'Why this crying and commotion? The child is not dead: she is asleep.' But they only laughed at him. After turning all the others out, he took the child's father and mother and his own companions and went in where the child was lying. Then, taking hold of her hand, he said to her, 'Talitha cum', which means, 'Get up, my child.' Immediately the girl got up and walked about – she was twelve years old. At that they were beside themselves with amazement. He gave them strict orders to let no one hear about it, and told them to give her something to eat." Mark v. 21–24, 35–43.

Also read: Matthew ix. 18–19, 23–26, Luke viii. 41–42, 49–56.

57

THIS INCIDENT shows the popularity that our Lord enjoyed, for a time at least, and bears witness to the astonishing healing power which He was able to exercise. He attributed this power to faith. The whole story illustrates the importance of belief.

The President of one of the synagogues begged Jesus to go with Him to his house to lay His hands on his twelve-year-old daughter who was thought to be dying. In this instance our Lord does not "speak the word only" to heal at a distance, as He did on other occasions.

It appears that almost every case of healing presented to us by the evangelists is different. Jesus consented to go to the house and He and the President were immediately surrounded by a jostling crowd.

On the way they received a message that the girl had died. At this the father seems to have been ready to abandon all hope but Jesus said, "Do not be afraid, only believe." Verse 37 in Mark perhaps means that the crowd also gave up hope of seeing a miracle and left Jesus to go on with the President and only three of His own disciples.

The importance of belief is so emphasized throughout the New Testament that perhaps we need to examine more closely the relation of our faith to the events of life. Our faith is what we actually believe in our inmost hearts and not of course what we *say* that we believe (e.g. in the recital of creeds) or even what we *think* we believe. Unless we do daily exercises in honesty of thought, confronting our minds for example with the word of God in Scripture or experience, we can easily deceive ourselves. What do I really believe about God? Does the spirit control the flesh, or does the flesh control the spirit? When the Church declares that Jesus is the Saviour of the world, what does that mean to me or to any intelligent person? Seeing that Jesus Himself suffered so much should Christians try to avoid suffering? These are among the questions that we need to answer as best we can to find out what we actually do believe about life. For our experience of life will be in accordance with our deep beliefs.

Arrived at the house they found that the professional mourners were already in possession. This ostentatious and mercenary grief may seem shocking to us though it is not without parallel in contemporary society and was the usual convention of the time.

There seems no reason why the words of our Lord should not be taken literally when He assured the family that the girl was not dead but asleep or unconscious. In the absence of a qualified physician the family would be unable to distinguish between death and coma. There would not be much practical difference between the two as the girl would undoubtedly have become a victim of premature burial (so frequent in the East) if she had not been rescued by Jesus.

But even our Lord did not attempt to restore this girl to health until He had removed from the scene the people who were drenching the whole atmosphere with their dismal, negative thoughts. Faith must protect itself from the false suggestions by which we are always surrounded. (See Rom. xii. 2.)

Wherever any good work is being done there are sure to be people whose presence makes its accomplishment more difficult, not by active opposition but by the doubt and pessimism which they generate. To show any impatience or hostility to such people would only add to the poison already in the atmosphere, but they must be kindly yet firmly dealt with. Usually they mean no harm. They are only trying to be informative or perhaps sympathetic. To ignore or make light of a neighbour's suffering would seem unfeeling, so instead they make the most of it, not realising that in so doing they are making it worse.

There are others who seem to feel that it is to their credit as sensitive, human persons to make conversation about all the more grisly events in the current news, dwelling on the sufferings of the innocent and the baffling injustices of life. When this becomes a habit it can only result in the corroding of faith. No one who constantly talks and thinks in such a way as to hint at the incompetence or negligence of God can expect to have much power in prayer.

But the converse is also true. When we respond to the appeal *change your minds and believe the good news*, when we are *called out of darkness into light*, we are changed from being bad citizens into good neighbours to all, and from being anti-social liabilities into positive helpers of each other's faith. Faith, be it remembered, is a primary necessity not only for religion but also for life, and whether we like it or not what we think in our inmost heart makes us what we are.

All human beings without exception have faith of some kind. Either they believe in good or they believe in evil. Perhaps most of us believe in a mixture of both. Up to a point we believe in Christ but we're not sure just how far our faith should go!

We must never forget those of whom the prophet said, "I will bring evil upon this people even the fruit of their thoughts" (Jer. vi. 19). On the other hand we could say with confidence, my future health and prosperity, or my usefulness to all who know me, will be the fruit of my thoughts, even if it takes some time to ripen.

Why did our Lord take with Him Peter and James and John, the three disciples whom He chose as His companions on several important occasions? It could hardly have been because these were the men who best understood Him and shared His vision of the Kingdom of God, for the gospels frankly record their failure to grasp His purpose or to enter into the spirit of His ministry (Mark viii. 33: x. 35–45, John xii. 16). It was only after His death that they began to see the meaning of much that He had said and done. Even so they loved Him with the kind of love which finds expression in obedience. They were His special friends and good companions and Jesus knew that He could trust them to be helpful both in speech and silence. There are such whose presence creates something of goodwill and serenity and the calm expectation of good. Could it be that their presence was just as necessary for the working of this miracle as was the absence of those who had been put out?

The importance of an atmosphere of prayer or a fellowship of faith for healing must not be overlooked. A woman scientist had been invited to give a talk to a group of Quakers. When the day of her lecture came she was suffering from a sudden attack of influenza. Not wishing to disappoint her audience she drove to the meeting house in which the lecture was to be given, but in the time of silence which preceded her talk she felt so ill that she decided there was nothing for it but to make an apology and beg someone present to drive her home. As she rose to do so, however, she felt better and almost to her own surprise found herself beginning her lecture with some enthusiasm. It was only after answering a number of questions and during the closing silence that she remembered her illness – to find that it was gone. None of the distressing symptoms she had felt an hour earlier remained. She drove home saying to herself, "How very odd, I'm perfectly well!" On thinking it over she attributed her sudden recovery to the silent prayer by which she had been surrounded.

Every Christian congregation should be such a fellowship of faith and prayer that any person coming into it must, from the spiritual atmosphere that it creates, receive some appreciable benefit. There is mounting evidence of a healing power known and used in antiquity as it is to-day. To dismiss it as incredible because at present we are still unable to explain it is the part not of intelligence but rather of inverted superstition. Many years ago Dr. Alexis Carrel writing of the "many marvellous cases" of healing which he considered to be modern miracles said: "This mass of phenomena introduces us into a new world, the exploration of which has not begun and will be fertile in surprises. What we already know for certain is that prayer produces tangible effects. However strange this may appear we must consider as true that whosoever asks receives, and that the door is opened to him who knocks"![1]

[1] *Prayer*, by Dr. Alexis Carrel, Hodder & Stoughton.

X

THE WOMAN WHO TOUCHED JESUS

"AMONG them was a woman who had suffered from haemorrhages for twelve years; and in spite of long treatment by doctors, on which she had spent all she had, there had been no improvement; on the contrary, she had grown worse. She had heard what people were saying about Jesus; so she came up from behind in the crowd and touched his cloak; for she said to herself, 'If I touch even his clothes, I shall be cured.' And there and then the source of her haemorrhages dried up and she knew in herself that she was cured of her trouble. At the same time Jesus, aware that power had gone out of him, turned round in the crowd and asked, 'Who touched my clothes?' His disciples said to him, 'You see the crowd pressing upon you and yet you ask, "Who touched me?"' Meanwhile he was looking round to see who had done it. And the woman, trembling with fear when she grasped what had happened to her, came and fell at his feet and told him the whole truth. He said to her, 'My daughter, your faith has cured you. Go in peace, free for ever from this trouble."' Mark v. 25–34.

Also read: Matthew ix. 20–22, Luke viii. 43–48.

WE HAVE considered cases in which our Lord touched sick people and so healed them. This is the case of someone who touched Jesus and was healed. The disorder here described is not unknown to modern psychotherapy which records at least one instantaneous cure also as a result of touch.[1]

This cure is another instance of faith. The sick woman had

[1] See *How to Pray for Healing*, James Clarke & Co.

63

kept saying to herself, "If I can only touch His clothes I shall be put right." She may have known nothing about Jesus except that He had power to heal and so she got into the crowd that was following Him and pushed her way closer and closer to Him.

She had reason to be nervous. Her malady made her ritually unclean and therefore untouchable (Lev. xv. 25–30). But she was driven by sheer need. She had once been a woman of some means and perhaps something remained of the personal fortune that she had spent in vain attempts to recover her health. It must not be taken for granted that she was the lowly, shrinking creature that has been imagined. She may rather have been of the imperious disposition that is used to getting what it wants at all costs. Whatever her character she was determined to get well.

Her immediate discovery by the feeling of loss of power on the part of Jesus, is a curious fact about which we should like to know more. Is verse 30 of Mark the explanation offered by our Lord Himself or by the evangelist? The woman, who had hoped to escape notice, was now more scared than ever by the realization that she had in fact been healed and could no longer conceal herself. Jesus in a reassuring word attributed her cure to her own faith and confirmed it by word.

How did this woman come to have such faith in Jesus? Perhaps she had watched Him for days before she dared get near Him. Perhaps it was the appearance of Jesus that inspired her confidence. The nature of her illness suggests that she had once been assaulted by a bad man. Now she had met and touched One whom she recognised to be a supremely good Man. Perhaps that was all she knew. But even such a simple and uninstructed faith was sufficient to admit the power of God to heal.

The curious feature of this act of healing is that it seems, as far as our Lord was aware, to have happened involuntarily, without any word or touch on His part, and without His conscious consent. He did not profess to know of the healing until it had been accomplished, and even then He did not know who had been healed.

Can there be such impersonal healing? Certainly there can, and there are many instances of it, though they do not all support some favourite theories. Naaman the leper, when he bathed repeatedly in the Jordan, was healed of his scabies, largely through his faith in the reputation of the prophet who prescribed the treatment, though the properties of the Jordan water doubtless had something to do with it. Many ancient relics which were said to have healing power lived up to their reputation which was maintained by the simple faith of the sick people who touched them and were healed. A successful pilgrimage to Lourdes is largely dependent on such childlike faith, such as our Lord commended, though here there is also to be taken into consideration the effect of prolonged prayer.

A young woman who was suffering from a troublesome illness which no treatment had so far been able to relieve went to worship in a Free Church not far from London. Something in the preacher inspired her confidence and at the close of the service she ran to him and seizing his hand she clung to him for a moment saying, "Hold me please, hold me!" The minister was taken by surprise but seeing the girl's earnestness he laid his hand on her in blessing. Shortly afterwards her doctor certified that she had been healed.

The power of mind is immense and it can be used for both good and evil. What a whole community expects to happen is almost sure to do so unless some other strong influence is at work to counteract the general belief. Even the wholehearted conviction of one person, undiminished by any divided mind, can achieve wonders. This incident is a record of the power of simple faith and expectation of good and reminds us of one element which is perhaps always present in any kind of healing.

Even the highly skilled surgeon and experienced physician count on this disposition to recover health, the absence of which may frustrate the use of even the best treatments.

The faith of the woman who was cured of haemorrhage may have been so simple as to be almost crude. Eusebius, the Church historian, records a legend that she was a Gentile from Caesarea-Philippi where she afterwards erected a statue to commemorate her healing. Her belief in God may therefore have been no more enlightened than that of many among us today. But she did believe in Jesus. There is no evidence that she had accepted His teaching or became His disciple. But perhaps like thousands more she had been attracted to the Man who was so different from all others, for reasons which she could not have explained even to herself.

XI

HE MAKES EVERYTHING NEW

"On his return journey from Syrian territory he went by way of Sidon to the Sea of Galilee through the territory of the Ten Towns. They brought to him a man who was deaf and had an impediment in his speech, with the request that he would lay his hand on him. He took the man aside, away from the crowd, put his fingers into his ears, spat, and touched his tongue. Then, looking up to heaven, he sighed, and said to him, '*Ephphatha*', which means 'Be opened'. With that his ears were opened, and at the same time the impediment was removed and he spoke plainly. Jesus forbade them to tell anyone; but the more he forbade them, the more they published it. Their astonishment knew no bounds: 'All that he does, he does well,' they said; 'he even makes the deaf hear and the dumb speak.' "
Mark vii. 31–37.

Also read: Matthew xv. 29–31.

THIS INCIDENT disposes of the question, Is faith in the healing power of God compatible with the use of such medical treatment as is in vogue? When we pray for the sick, committing them to the care of God, and taking into our minds on their behalf His power to heal as it was seen in Jesus, we are praying also for all the means used for their recovery, and for the guidance and inspiration of all who attend to their needs. God will use the doctor and nurse and the treatment they administer as He will use our prayers to accomplish His own will. The fact that complete recovery of health has often been

67

known to occur where no other treatment but prayer was available does not indicate that faith in God excludes faith in His gifts of medicine and skill.

This is a very interesting case of healing, all the more so because it seems to modify belief in Jesus as a divine Healer who could cure infirmity with a word or a touch. In this instance of healing our Lord acts more like a skilled physician who makes use of known remedies and applies them to the patient in a treatment which takes an appreciable time to become effective. Perhaps it is for this reason that Matthew, who is following Mark's version here, passes over this miracle, substituting for it three verses in which he gives a general account of our Lord's wonderful power to heal all kinds of ailments, picking up Mark's narrative again at the feeding of the multitude.

We have already observed that our Lord used different methods of healing in different cases. The power of God to heal all kinds of sickness is not in question, but some sufferers can receive it more immediately than others. This deaf and dumb man brought forward by eager friends, may have known little about Jesus. Our Lord graciously stopped to help the man in the condition in which he was, and used such popular, if to us crude, remedies as the patient might expect. Tacitus[1] describes the use of similar means of healing. Are there people who can be healed only by such treatments as they understand and believe in? Perhaps in another two thousand years people will look back upon the drugs and surgery which are in common use today as very primitive means of healing. But these are the means in which this century believes and perhaps for many sufferers they are the only way to health.

An interesting comment on the value of material means for healing was made by a distinguished physician who said: (the quotation is from memory) "I believe that there are powers, mental or psychic or divine, which can be used in healing, and

[1] History, iv. 81.

some day scientific research will bring to light as yet undiscovered laws of nature which may be used to heal and prevent diseases. These powers are at present only partially understood and until we know more about them, should be used with caution. I believe", he went on to say, "in telepathy and in the power of human minds under certain circumstances to communicate with each other without any material means. Some day perhaps we shall all be so trained in these quite simple, but as yet unexplored, faculties that we can put the General Post Office out of business. Meantime I prefer to use the telephone. In another hundred years there may be very great changes in the treatment of disease and possibly the emphasis now placed on material healing may shift to spiritual. Meantime I would advise patients to put their trust in the known and accepted remedies which have proved their worth."

There is a right and a wrong way of using medicines and other material means in healing. They can be made a substitute for a more profound treatment or they can be the means by which the healing power of God is conveyed to the patient. If we do not want to know what truly is wrong with us, and snatch at anything that will relieve our discomfort or pain to impart temporary stimulant, we may be turning away from something that God is showing us about ourselves and our real needs. But if we are willing to come to terms with life as it is and to face the spiritual as well as the material facts of our condition, then the gifts of God in medicine may be like a sacrament which uses the tangible as the vehicle of the intangible.

In all healing a correct diagnosis is of the first importance. A good physician is not content to look at the surface or to treat the symptoms only. He examines the patient to discover the nature of his illness and the means by which he can be made whole. Your accident was not just bad luck or somebody's incompetence, and your recurring bouts of influenza are not due only to the weather or a prevalent virus. Most sicknesses are symptoms of a spiritual condition which can be healed only by spiritual means.

It will be noted again that our Lord in this case took the patient aside from the crowd. The common mind is always a potent source of good or evil, and both its credulity and its incredulity must be taken into account. Again the patient when healed is warned not to talk about his healing.

The sufferer was deaf and dumb and a curious word is used to describe his inability to speak, and recalls, perhaps intentionally, the Greek version (Septuagint) of Isaiah xxxv. 5.

Why did Jesus sigh? It is another of those Markan touches of human feeling by which this evangelist portrays His character. Perhaps the treatment had taken longer than the brief narrative suggests, and it was a sigh of weariness or relief. Could it be that the deaf and dumb man was not a very good patient and was inclined to resist the healing power of Christ? Or perhaps it was just a sigh of prayer or of thanksgiving. It was after the treatment had been given that the spoken word of prayer, *Ephphatha, be opened*, finally dismissed the infirmity.

Intercessory prayer could be regarded as working together with Christ. We realise that He who "ever liveth to make intercession" is ceaselessly active in every situation of need to heal and to bless, and that our part is to serve Him and co-operate with Him. Sometimes the desired recovery of health may not come immediately and then we must not lose heart or suppose that our prayers are in vain. Even Jesus on occasion had to deal patiently with conditions that resisted His power and sighed in prayer as He laboured to complete His healing work. We must never give up. "Men ought always to pray and not to faint" (Luke xviii. i.), and perhaps it was to encourage us in persistent prayer that the evangelist included this story of healing by prolonged treatment.

A woman in the North of England (who is still living with her husband in excellent health and remarkably active for her age) was many years ago taken ill with a serious complaint which her doctor for a time treated unsuccessfully. At last she was taken to a specialist who declared that she was suffering from a disease for which (at that time) there was no known cure. The specialist, himself a devout Christian, while very sincerely advising the patient and her husband that there was no hope of recovery through medical means, advised them to seek the help of their church in prayer. This was done and after some months, though no other treatment was used, the patient's condition began to improve. Gradually the symptoms disappeared until after nearly two years during which meditative prayer for health was practised constantly the woman had regained her normal health. Had she and her husband, not to say the local church, been more experienced in healing prayer the recovery might have been more rapid, and perhaps almost instantaneous. But though the process of healing was slow it was none the less one of those "miracles" of which modern life is just as full as are the Gospels.

XII

BARTIMEUS

"THEY came to Jericho; and as he was leaving the town, with his disciples and a large crowd, Bartimaeus, son of Timaeus, a blind beggar, was seated at the roadside. Hearing that it was Jesus of Nazareth, he began to shout, 'Son of David, Jesus, have pity on me!' Many of the people rounded on him: 'Be quiet,' they said; but he shouted all the more, 'Son of David, have pity on me.' Jesus stopped and said, 'Call him'; so they called the blind man and said, 'Take heart; stand up; he is calling you.' At that he threw off his cloak, sprang up, and came to Jesus. Jesus said to him, 'What do you want me to do for you?' 'Master,' the blind man answered, 'I want my sight back.' Jesus said to him, 'Go; your faith has cured you!' And at once he recovered his sight and followed him on the road." Mark x. 46–52.

Also read: Matthew xx. 29–34, Luke xviii. 35–43.

BLINDNESS is prevalent in the Middle East and may have been more so in the time of our Lord. Among its causes are sunglare, flying dust and trachoma, but there are often psychological causes too. In modern times many soldiers confronted by revolting sights in war have been temporarily and sometimes permanently blinded. This is the work of a merciful and unconscious nature to spare them the pain of sensations and memories that might prove unbearable. The same experience can happen to victims of accidents when sudden functional blindness protects from the horror of witnessing a fatal injury, perhaps to a loved one. A contributory cause of blindness is sometimes an unconscious reluctance to see on the part of the sufferer. Blindness is bad, but to face reality may seem to some people even more trying, and there are those who sometimes have found in the failing or loss of sight an excuse for failure which otherwise would be intolerable.

The story of Bartimeus is another which is packed with human interest. The narrative in Mark, who alone gives the beggar's name, seems to imply that Bartimeus was a familiar figure. He heard the footsteps of a large crowd and on enquiry heard that Jesus of Nazareth was passing by. So popular was our Lord during this period of His ministry that He could go nowhere without crowds surrounding Him. Even Bartimeus had heard of Him and had called to Him for help. The crowd, probably supposing that Bartimeus was merely begging as usual, told him to be quiet, but he persisted in shouting to Jesus to take pity on him. He called Jesus "Son of David" which could be a Messianic title but, as Bartimeus used it, was probably only a complimentary form of address. A beggar to-day could call a man "Guvnor" without the imputation that he governed anything.

In response to this continued loud appeal Jesus stood still and said, "Call him to come". Now the crowd changed its attitude to Bartimeus. "Buck up," they said, "He's calling for you." Bartimeus threw off his outer garment and jumping up was pushed forward to where Jesus stood.

"What do you want me to do for you?" said Jesus.

"Lord," said Bartimeus, "give me back my sight." Our Lord used the word that means both to save and to heal. "Go, your faith has saved you", He said. What does it mean to be saved? As he mixed in the crowd that was following Jesus, Bartimeus knew, not in doctrine, but in fact.

The question that our Lord put to Bartimeus was not redundant. What did he want? For some people prayer is only a kind of begging. They call upon their God for help, but without any clear notion of what they expect God to do. Much prayer is far too vague to be effective. Do you imagine that after you have been praying for a while, if you stopped to listen, you would hear the Lord saying, "Now what *do* you want me to do for you?"

A great deal of what is called "unanswered prayer" could be traced to uncertainty of asking. "The double-minded man, unstable in all his ways" gets little sympathy from St. James (i. 7) who says bluntly, "let not that man suppose that he shall receive anything of the Lord." This does not mean that we are not to seek the help of God in making up our minds. A large part of our prayers may be taken up by the attempt to find out what we really want from life. Many people express a devout desire to discover the will of God; they would soon find out if they put themselves unreservedly under His guidance and then waited to see what God will do. But God, who is love, does not enforce His will. He offers it as a loving Father and calls us into co-operation in the working out of His purpose. The question for all who pray must be, Do I really want the will of God? Or has this phrase come to mean little more than what *I am* determined should happen?

Prayer could be described as committing our heart's desire to the divine power so that it may be put into effect. But if we do not know our heart's desire or know it so vaguely or inconsistently that our prayers become a mass of contradictions, the divine power that could answer a definite prayer decisively can only establish and enlarge the incoherence of our minds.

One of the most important obligations of life is to get to know what we want. Many a life is futile because it has no motive or vocation. Many a prayer is impotent because it asks for nothing. The high roads of life are full of beggars craving help with no notion of the kind of help they want, blind to the nature of their own real needs. Their hearts ache for love, for recognition, for a cause to serve and a Lord to worship and they beg for a copper.

It is the voice of God that is saying to us in all patience, with no reproach (he giveth to all men liberally upbraiding not), What do you want me to do for you? There can be no question of His power to help or His willingness to do so. How often we make His alleged reluctance to give, an excuse for our own unwillingness to ask!

One part of faith is decision to take what God has promised. Many good people are almost afraid to ask lest He might not be able to grant their request, and that would be embarrassing for all. I recall a meeting at which a very considerate chairman refused a question because he thought the speaker could not answer it, and so the meeting sang a hymn instead! How like that type of piety that will not ask God for too much lest He should not be able to meet the demand! Faith asks and it asks much but never as much as God yearns to give.

Are our prayers big enough or are we content to ask like beggars for gratuities?

> Thou art coming to a king,
> Large petitions with thee bring.

Bartimeus knew what he wanted. As a beggar his blindness was his stock in trade, but he wanted his sight. He is not the only one whose infirmity is his chief claim to sympathy. But he had faith to see that his prayer could be answered not by a passing gesture of pity but by a new life of health and liberty and service to his fellow men.

XIII

TREES WALKING

"THEY arrived at Bethsaida. There the people brought a blind man to Jesus and begged him to touch him. He took the blind man by the hand and led him away out of the village. Then he spat on his eyes, laid his hands upon him, and asked whether he could see anything. The man's sight began to come back, and he said, 'I see men; they look like trees, but they are walking about.' Jesus laid his hands on his eyes again; he looked hard, and now he was cured so that he saw everything clearly. Then Jesus sent him home, saying, 'Do not tell anyone in the village.'" Mark viii. 22–26.

THIS INCIDENT at Bethsaida is so similar in vocabulary to that recorded in Mark vii. 31–37 that some scholars regard it as another version of the same event. Both record an instance of gradual healing. In both Jesus uses the popular if primitive remedy of spittle and the laying on of hands. In both the healing is followed by a stern injunction to say nothing about it.

The two stories, however, have certain peculiarities which distinguish them from each other. It is hard to believe that our Lord's unusual enquiry (it is the only occasion on which He is said to have asked such a question in the course of a treatment) in verse 23, "Can you see anything?", or the blind man's answer, "I can see men: they look like trees walking" is not a genuine reminiscence that has no parallel in the report of any other miracle.

This is another case in which healing was not instantaneous

76

but the result of carefully applied treatment. It has been supposed that the brief account given by the evangelist could conceal or perhaps suggest that our Lord worked for some time on the patient before the cure was completed, as perhaps He did in the case of the Deaf-Mute in Mark vii. 31. From both these records it appears that, far from the effortless authority or the touch of compassion with which other miracles of healing were immediately accomplished, in these two instances of healing recorded by Mark, Jesus had to go to work on the sick man with energy as well as skill, and that it was not without prolonged effort and care that He restored them to health.

Neither Matthew nor Luke have found a place in their Gospels for these miracles. They preferred to record cases which they considered to be a more striking tribute to the healing power of Christ. But does healing that requires patience and care give less glory to God than such immediate cures as are recorded alike by the Gospels and by modern medicine? There are as many different kinds of treatment as there are diseases – perhaps as many as there are patients – and some apparently simple cures may take as much solicitude and skill as release from long-standing infirmities. It is not that the healing power of God is sometimes less, but that human resistance to it is sometimes more.

We can readily believe that our Lord possessed an intellect and faith that were able to put the healing power of God into effect with a spontaneity that defies the normal limits of human nature. It may be, as some suppose, that in the Gospels there is a tendency to exaggerate the spectacular authority with which Jesus on occasion commanded and controlled the diseases that afflicted the people. Even so, exaggeration usually points to something so wonderful that it seemed to call for such excited description. All miracles are not alike. There are instances of infirmity which our Lord confronted not by a display of overwhelming power, but rather by a long consideration and a humble trust that led the patient away into a quiet place and there nursed him back to health. Even when Jesus was the healer the sickness did not always go like a flash, or the exorcism of an evil spirit, but rather step by step from one state of improvement to another until the invalid was quite restored.

Is such gradual recovery less wonderful or less to the glory of God than instantaneous healing? Suppose it were not an instance of bodily healing but of that change of character which is called "conversion". A sudden conversion like that of St. Paul on the road to Damascus is a striking act of God. But we have seen lives changed not so dramatically but quite as effectually by the action of divine grace over a period of time. Is it because, perhaps in the case of Paul of Tarsus, there was a time of preparation, a time of resistance to God which the gentle persuasion of divine love had to overcome? Does the love of God, which by its very nature must insist on the freedom of the soul, forbear to compel by an irresistible grace the moral personality of any man but allows the mind estranged from God time to change of its own accord? The result may seem to be a sudden transformation but the change may nevertheless have been long in ripening. Just as the blossom bursts out as it were overnight on a spring morning and appears to our astonished vision a miracle of nature. Yet the sudden outburst is the conclusion of slow processes and patient growth.

Healing, like conversion, may be instantaneous. In that moment of truth we realise that God is reigning and that nothing withstands His perfect will except the resistance of our own minds; then the barriers are swept away and the power of God flows through. We have seen it happening in modern life as well as in the Gospels. But sometimes our emotional opposition to the will of God, or it may be some natural obstruction to the divine power within us, takes longer to yield. It is no fancy that we are all affected more or less by the false beliefs and disturbed emotional content of the community in which we live, and it may be that what might otherwise be an instantaneous act of God may appear as a gradual process.

For all of us who pray and work for the healing of the people is it not an encouragement to learn that even in the experience of our blessed Lord the achievement of God's will in the recovery of health may take time and skill as well as earnest endeavour? At Edward Wilson House we know personally several men and women who at one time were victims of diseases for which the medical science of the time could offer no cure, but who now, as a result of prolonged meditative prayer, are restored to health and are living an active life in the service of Christ. The power which led them to recovery could doubtless, if we had been able to receive it, have healed them instantly. But the divine power, mediated as it is through the imperfect prayers of man, can do only gradually and slowly, what the Master of Faith could have accomplished instantly. Is the daily progress to health through months of patient hope and trust less wonderful and less thank-worthy than the sudden healing which in point of time seems more miraculous? We have seen recoveries which to all appearances were almost instantaneous and we have watched diseases, for which at the time there was said to be no cure, gradually disappear through months of prayer. Both are the Lord's doing and marvellous in our eyes.

For historic instances of the use of touch and saliva see Dr. Leslie Weatherhead: *Psychology, Religion and Healing*, Hodder & Stoughton, p. 56.

XIV

THE EPILEPTIC BOY

"WHEN they came back to the disciples they saw a crowd surrounding them and lawyers arguing with them. As soon as they saw Jesus the whole crowd were overcome with awe, and they ran forward to welcome him. He asked them, 'What is this argument about?' A man in the crowd spoke up: 'Master, I brought my son to you. He is possessed by a spirit which makes him speechless. Whenever it attacks him, it dashes him to the ground, and he foams at the mouth, grinds his teeth, and goes rigid. I asked your disciples to cast it out, but they failed.' Jesus answered: 'What an unbelieving and perverse generation! How long shall I be with you? How long must I endure you? Bring him to me.' So they brought the boy to him; and as soon as the spirit saw him it threw the boy into convulsions, and he fell on the ground and rolled about foaming at the mouth. Jesus asked his father, 'How long has he been like this?' 'From childhood,' he replied; 'often it has tried to make an end of him by throwing him into the fire or into water. But if it is at all possible for you, take pity upon us and help us.' 'If it is possible!' said Jesus. 'Everything is possible to one who has faith.' 'I have faith,' cried the boy's father; 'help me where faith falls short.' Jesus saw then that the crowd was closing in upon them, so he rebuked the unclean spirit. 'Deaf and dumb spirit,' he said, 'I command you, come out of him and never go back!' After crying aloud and racking fiercely, it came out; and the boy looked like a corpse; in fact, many said, 'He is dead.' But Jesus took his hand and raised him to his feet, and he stood up.

"Then Jesus went indoors, and his disciples asked him privately,

'Why could not we cast it out?' He said, 'There is no means of casting out this sort but prayer.' " Mark ix. 14–29.
Also read: Matthew xvii. 14–21, Luke ix. 37–43.

O F ALL HEALING miracles this is one of the most appealing. The alarming condition of the boy, the natural anxiety of the father and his conflicting faith and fear, together with the inability of the disciples to effect a cure, intensify the human interest of the story. Our Lord's outspoken disappointment in the lack of faith of the people and of His own disciples is especially noteworthy.

Most commentators understand that the symptoms described indicate some form of epilepsy. The Markan record, closely followed but abbreviated by both Matthew and Luke, makes it clear that our Lord was perfectly assured of the power of God to heal disease however grave the symptoms, and that He expected His disciples to transmit this power as He Himself did. The secret of this power is faith. *All things are possible to him that believeth* (Mark ix. 23).

But is this saying of our Lord to be understood literally or is it not a somewhat theoretical statement? Does it mean, a man of faith can overcome the greatest obstacles in the achievement of his aspirations? Faith is a very great help in any high endeavour. The great explorers, inventors and benefactors of humanity have been people of faith. All this we can heartily believe. But did our Lord mean more than this? Did He suggest that in any situation of need immediate and sufficient help from heaven is available to those who believe in it?

If so, why are we so often helpless in the face of disaster? Why must we watch loved ones suffering, and often dying of some foul disease, while we stand by impotent to save them? Why must the whole community and even the Church be poisoned by selfish ambitions, envy and jealousy, hypocrisy and greed while even the redeeming love of God seems ineffective to control the unruly passions of men despite our constant prayers?

That our Lord did indeed utter these words just as they are recorded, and that He meant exactly what He said, becomes the more convincing when we compare this saying with others to a like effect. *With men*, He said on one occasion, *this is impossible, but not with God, for with God all things are possible*. Probably on more than one occasion He declared, *According to your faith be it unto you*, laying it down as a law of life that events will take the shape of our convictions. There is much also that Jesus said about prayer which goes beyond the practice of the Church in any age. When we put together all this teaching, and add no qualification, we get the impression that He believed, and meant His disciples to believe, that there is no trouble in life that will not yield to persistent trust in God.

Then why was He Himself a Man of Sorrows? Why did He suffer every pain and indignity and humiliation as recorded in the Gospels? Why did He, dying on the Cross, cry out in bitterest anguish *My God, my God, why hast thou forsaken me?* (Psalm xxii. 1). The crucifixion of our Lord, and all that it meant of suffering and sorrow, was an event which, so far from trying to escape as though it were a misfortune, He regarded as a necessity for the achievement of His divine mission. He set His face steadfastly, says Luke, to go up to Jerusalem (Luke ix. 51). He repeatedly warned His disciples that He must suffer betrayal and death, and so fulfil the prophetic ideal of one who would redeem His people by vicarious suffering. It is true that in the agony in Gethsemane He shrank from the dreadful consummation of His ministry of which He had earlier made irrevocable choice, but His natural prayer that He might be spared what was to come ended in the triumph of faith. *Nevertheless not my will but thine be done* (Mark xiv. 36). The crucifixion is not something that happened in spite of our Lord's trust in God, but because of it. The appearance of weakness was the reality of power, and He knew it. The Cross might be described as the supreme act of faith of all time. It became possible, with all its consequences, for the salvation of the world, through our Lord's belief in God and in the power of creative suffering.

On the other hand it is not hard to see that sickness and sorrow and much of the pain and suffering of life are often the product of belief. A man is taken ill and after a time is pronounced to be incurable. He is not told of the gravity of his condition lest his morale should suffer and his resistance to disease be weakened, but his family know and presently the whole community in which he lives has begun to mourn for him. The news that he has not long to live causes genuine distress among his loved ones and friends who, though they bravely keep up their spirits, cannot but contemplate the unhappy future which they know to be inevitable. When prayers are said in the church the effect is like that of the celebration of the last rites and now everybody believes that the invalid has not long to live. According to their belief it happens. In the end it is what we believe that is the only possibility.

Our very compassion for those who suffer, together with a laudable reluctance to appear unsympathetic, often make complete frankness very difficult. We would not all wish to be like the Irish priest who, after having visited the sick room of one of his parishioners, came down to find the family gathered in gloomy expectation of the worst and burst out, "He isn't dying of cancer – he's dying of your unbelief"! But is there perhaps a truth in our Lord's utterance that we often fail to realise? How much does our belief contribute to the situation in which we find ourselves? Have we too readily sided with secular opinion and taken up the attitude of those who have no real faith in God? Perhaps it is no fault of ours that we cannot always break through the prevalent unfaith of our times. Even our Lord it seems could not always do that (Matt. xiii. 58). There were communities in which, as Matthew tells us, the divine power in Christ was thwarted by the popular scepticism.

Most of us feel, as the father of this epileptic boy felt, that we do believe, and we want to know how we can believe more than we do. We cannot force ourselves to believe; that would be mere dishonesty. Faith is increased by looking at the truth, especially by quiet waiting upon God in meditation. Conviction comes from study of the evidence and the more we look towards God the more we believe in Him. Even the imperfect faith of this father sufficed to enable Jesus to heal his son.

When the disciples demanded to know why their attempts to heal the boy were unavailing they got no sympathy from Jesus, who (according to Matthew) said frankly *Because of your unbelief*. Is that what He would say to us when we want to know why our prayers have not been answered? The disciples themselves were apparently disappointed, as indeed they might be after their experience recorded in Luke x. 17. This is probably the right place for this emphatic statement of the power of faith which the evangelists place in different contexts (Mark xi. 23; Luke xvii. 6).

Perhaps just here we should stop to ask, But what is meant in the New Testament by faith? To begin with we can see that faith of the kind that puts the power of God into action is not just an impulsive assent to the suggestion that there is more in life than we can understand. It is the deep conviction that God is in control, that the universe has been created by His *word* or *thought;* that material things have their origin in spiritual. A thorough-going materialist, as so many of our generation are, cannot easily shake off the mental habits of a lifetime. Sudden conversions are not impossible, but we have to change our minds and believe the good news before we can see the Reign of Heaven of which our Lord said His healing miracles were signs. Faith is, therefore, an understanding of life. It is a response to the Spirit, an appreciation of spiritual values. If our way of life makes it abundantly clear to all that we put our trust entirely in material things, and seek our security and health and happiness from the abundance of material things, it will be hard for us in the hour of crisis suddenly to exercise that trust in the unseen and eternal which is faith.

Faith is not so much the acceptance of a creed as a way of life. We declare our beliefs not so convincingly in what we say as by what we are. Without listening to a word we say, anyone who knows us can tell how much we believe in Christ by our manner of living, which after all is our true religion.

Does this criterion condemn us all as faithless? It does indeed, yet it is not by achievement that we are judged but by the faith which shows through even our failures and our faults. There is all the difference in the world between trusting in ourselves that we are righteous, and trusting in the righteousness of Christ.

Another element in faith is immunity from the superstitions and errors to which worldly society, however otherwise sophisticated, still clings. There are many beliefs for which there is no foundation in either common sense or prophetic vision which nevertheless are almost taken for granted by millions of apparently educated people. It is as if some worldwide confidence trickster had perpetrated on humanity an enormous hoax for which most of us have fallen. On the analogy of the now ubiquitous machine the human body is supposed to be a contraption fitted together by a clever mechanic consisting of various bits and pieces which inevitably in the course of time wear out and, unless replaced by spares, will eventually perish on the scrap heap. The idea of the human body as the temple of the Holy Spirit and the creation, moment by moment of the invisible master-mind of the Eternal, if recalled at all, is only dismissed as the quaint relic of a primitive past. Or consider the prevalent fallacy that what man possesses is more important than what possesses man; or the fever that has stricken most of the Western world of perpetual motion and the pathetic faith in salvation by machine. How exciting are the exploits of man, bad or good – how fascinating his accomplishments, even his failures, whereas the work of God, if anyone has time to notice it, is brought into consideration only when all else has failed.

When our Lord said that life deals with us in accordance with our beliefs He was stating a law of nature for which the world is full of evidence. Our beliefs make us what we are; not of course the beliefs we profess but what we believe deep down in our hearts. If we believe that the world is a chancy jungle in which sorrow and sickness, violence and loss, treachery and error are constantly ready to pounce upon us, *that* is what life will be like for us. The kind of God we believe in determines the quality of our life.

Everything yields to faith, but some troubles are so stubborn that they demand the exercise of faith in prolonged prayer. We shall not of course be heard for our much speaking, nor for much meditation of the kind that is merely silent speech. But our Lord's own example indicates that sustained periods of prayer are desirable. Some teachers on prayer would say that we are all praying all the time for *something*, inasmuch as we habitually cherish desires in our hearts and these deep yearnings are our real prayers which never remain long unanswered. Others would say that it is in the instant in which our minds make contact with the divine Mind, in that moment of truth in which the channels of grace are opened by our realisation of the power of God, that the miracle happens in the transformation of the visible by the invisible. Even so, for most of us it may take prolonged waiting upon God to achieve just one such moment of vital communication with heaven. Faith is largely the renewing of our minds and the more vivid realisation of known truth. For that reason those are likely to be more helpful to their neighbours who make time for leisured prayer.

The last two words of v. 29 in Mark, 21 in Matthew, are

absent from some of the best manuscripts. Fasting in the sense of abstinence from food has very low religious value. But if it means the self-discipline of serious prayer we can see why the words were added in some versions.

Another case of healing by prayer only is that of an elderly man who suffered from some kind of eczema. Medical treatment would have been available but for the fact that the invalid's business necessitated constant travelling. He was instructed in the practice of affirmative and meditative prayer and within a few days the disease which had troubled him for months disappeared entirely. This proves nothing except the presence in nature (or in supernature, does it matter which?) of a healing power. If we can use it today is there any reason to deny that our Lord used it too?

XV

OBEDIENCE TO LAW

"When he had entered Capernaum a centurion came up to ask his help. 'Sir,' he said, 'a boy of mine lies at home paralysed and racked with pain.' Jesus said, 'I will come and cure him.' But the centurion replied, 'Sir, who am I to have you under my roof? You need only say the word and the boy will be cured. I know, for I am myself under orders, with soldiers under me. I say to one, "Go", and he goes; to another, "Come here", and he comes; and to my servant, "Do this", and he does it.' Jesus heard him with astonishment, and said to the people who were following him, 'I tell you this; nowhere, even in Israel, have I found such faith.'

"Then Jesus said to the centurion, 'Go home now; because of your faith, so let it be.' At that moment the boy recovered." Matthew viii. 5–13.

Also read: Luke vii. 1–10.

THE MIRACLES of healing recorded in the Gospels present to us a wide diversity of ministration. In the narrative now before us we have another illustration of healing by the spoken word.

All who are engaged in the ministry of healing must believe that in seeking to overcome the causes of disease and to promote health of spirit, soul and body they are working in obedience to the will of God. All the forces of nature are on their side. Sickness is an abnormality, a falling away from what ought to be, a failure in function or vitality, a deficiency or it may be an excess, but something that no healthy mind could desire for its own sake. The laws of God make for health and well-being. The physician endeavours to restore his patient to normality to as near an approach as may be to rightness and fitness. Whatever methods may be used to attain to this condition, those who seek it are working with powers that are present in life for the good of humanity.

Our Lord declared that when by casting out evil He healed the sick, that was evidence of divine action. "If I cast out devils by the Spirit of God then the Kingdom of God is come unto you." And He asked, "By whom do your children (physicians of your own persuasion) cast them out?" (Matt. xii. 27–28). In other words, is any kind of healing ever accomplished without co-operation with the Creator Spirit? The will of God is surely for the health of man. We bring troubles upon ourselves and our neighbours by disobedience, conscious or unconscious, to His perfect will.

The Centurion was one who had a simple faith in the sovereign will of God. Like others of his rank mentioned in the New Testament (Luke xxiii. 47; Acts x. 22; xxii. 26, xxiii. 17–23; xxiv. 23; xxvii. 43) he was doubtless an intelligent and good man as his concern for his slave indicates. He was probably not a proselyte but he had recognised the value of the Jewish religion by his generous gift of a synagogue. He was thus able to make a modest approach to Jesus through some of the leading Jewish citizens, who heartily commended to our Lord's attention his request for healing. Jesus consented and was on His way with them to the Centurion's house when He was intercepted by friends of the Centurion who begged Him not to take the trouble to come any further, but only to utter the word of command which the Centurion knew would be sufficient to restore his boy to health.

It may be that the words "I am not worthy . . ." mean "I am a Gentile and I understand that you as a Jew cannot enter my house without ceremonial defilement." In the account of Luke

vii. 6 the Centurion's friends courteously prevented Jesus from proceeding beyond the limits of religious propriety. Our Lord, however, recognised in this mark of consideration an additional sign of faith. This might look like excessive oriental courtesy, but presumably the Centurion was a Roman and he had Roman ideas of power. If an order was given by the Emperor in Rome he knew that it would be transmitted to all ranks by the appointed officers and implicitly obeyed. How much more if the Almighty gave an order in heaven would that order, transmitted through His appointed officers, become law which none dare resist!

This simple faith of the Centurion implied a profound trust which has often been mis-stated but, when rightly understood, works potently for good. It believes that nothing can withstand the will of God when it is fully accepted. The freedom that God gives us allows us to reject His will and to neglect it, but in the degree to which God's purpose is received in reverent self-surrender and unreserved obedience it will undoubtedly take effect in our lives.

It was this realisation of a law of life that is often ignored that won our Lord's high commendation. The Centurion cannot be claimed as a disciple of Christ. He reminds us of the fact that God's healing power is for all and not only for those who hold correct beliefs. Indeed many have been led to a deeper experience of faith through the experience of healing. This Roman soldier was perhaps a simple man, as many of his profession are. He had little knowledge of theology. But he believed in discipline and knew its necessity for the right ordering of society. If God was good, all you had to do was to obey Him, a point sometimes overlooked by those who are inclined to make discussion a substitute for obedience. Jesus is Saviour only when He is Lord.

Prayer is never an attempt to change God from what He is to something else, or His universe from what He has made to something different. God is perfect Being and any change in

His Mind or Will would be a change to imperfection. God is unchangeable for the simple reason that if He were to change He would cease to be God. We must not suppose that all this was in the Centurion's mind when he declared that healing was obedience to authority, but, however dimly, he did perceive this very important truth that in seeking health we must be obedient to the laws that God has made for our good.

People who come to ask for prayer sometimes reject the moral laws on which this ministry is based. Instead of submitting to God's law they want to lay down the law to God. "I will certainly not attend a prayer group led by a . . ." said one devout lady who believed that her religious principles could separate her from other Christians without separating her from Christ. "But it would be *wrong* to forgive them after all they've done", said a man who could not see the essential relation between healing and forgiveness, and who virtually believed that God had made a serious mistake in deciding to forgive sinners. The Centurion at least would not have succumbed to the temptation to rewrite the Gospel.

Prayer for healing, or any other religious ministry which has involved the restoration of persons to wholeness, puts into operation laws which God has ordained for our well-being. Prayer is God's act as well as ours, and far more than ours. If we do as God tells us God fulfils our need (John xv. 7). All we have to do is to fulfil the conditions which God has laid down.

One teacher of prayer who wrote at the beginning of this century whose work, though now superseded, has been used by a number of subsequent writers says: "We must not fly in the face of the Law by expecting it to do *for* us what it can only do *through* us; and we must therefore use our intelligence with the knowledge that it is acting *as the instrument of a greater Intelligence;* and because we have this knowledge we may, and should, cease from all anxiety as to the final result".[1]

[1] Judge Troward in *The Edinburgh Lectures.*

Just as neglect of God's laws can lead to sickness so observance of the royal law of love can lead to health. We are not
likely to be healed as long as we are indulging in a diet or a
way of life or some bad habit which is detrimental to health. We
need not, however, become the victims of enthusiasts who have
a panacea to sell, without the use of which, they are convinced,
all mankind will be lost. There are levels of life on which it is
more blessed to live than merely to be "fighting fit". What we
must remember is that our appeal to God for healing, whether
for ourselves or others, is always based on obedience to those
beneficent laws which God has ordained for our welfare. As the
epistle says: "To love God is to keep His laws and His laws are
not hard to keep. Every child of God thus overcomes the world.
The power that overcomes the world is our faith"[1] (1 John v.
3-4).

In prayer we are not ignoring the laws of God or trying to
evade them, but striving to put them into effect. Among the
laws of nature which science has not yet fully explored are those
in obedience to which the human mind is able to put into
operation powers which are capable of doing wonders, or as
some would say, working miracles. Miracles never happen in
defiance of God's laws but in observance of them.

[1] See also H. E. Fosdick's *The Meaning of Prayer* (S.C.M. Press), in chapter
entitled "Prayer and the Reign of Law".

XVI

A DAUGHTER OF ABRAHAM

"ONE Sabbath he was teaching in a synagogue, and there was a woman there possessed by a spirit that had crippled her for eighteen years. She was bent double and quite unable to stand up straight. When Jesus saw her he called her and said, 'You are rid of your trouble.' Then he laid his hands on her, and at once she straightened up and began to praise God. But the president of the synagogue, indignant with Jesus for healing on the Sabbath, intervened and said to the congregation, 'There are six working-days: come and be cured on one of them, and not on the Sabbath.' The Lord gave him his answer: 'What hypocrites you are!' he said. 'Is there a single one of you who does not loose his ox or his donkey from the manger and take it out to water on the Sabbath? And here is this woman, a daughter of Abraham, who has been kept prisoner by Satan for eighteen long years: was it wrong for her to be freed from her bond on the Sabbath?' At these words all his opponents were delighted at all the wonderful things he was doing." Luke xiii. 10–17.

THIS IS a very instructive instance of healing, for it gives us an insight into our Lord's regard for crippling infirmity, and shows how He used the laying on of hands. The passage has no parallel in the other Gospels and perhaps Luke preserved it because as a physician he was interested in our Lord's treatment of this kind of disease. Verse 11 shows that the condition of the woman was attributed by popular opinion to demonic possession, as all illness was. A spirit of infirmity is a spirit that causes infirmity, as a dumb spirit is one that causes dumbness.

It is not necessary to suppose that by *devils* or *evil spirits* the educated people of antiquity meant anything like what these words suggest today. The essence of their belief was that something which was not of the body had caused bodily harm. Undoubtedly there were superstitious people in our Lord's time, as in ours, but we must not read back into the Gospels medieval concepts of the devil which were not in vogue in the first century. What the Scripture says here is that the woman had been crippled by some influence that was more akin to the mind than to the body, or to the spirit than to the flesh.

Possession is a very frequent figure of speech used to indicate the presence in a person of a certain disposition or mind, or an attitude to life or way of thinking. In Philippians ii we read *Let that mind be in you which was also in Christ.* The writer means that something of the Christ spirit should be in us, or that we should become possessed by Christ as in Galatians ii. 20. The very contrary had happened to this unfortunate woman who was suffering from possession by a spirit or disposition not of Christ but of a quite different and contrary kind. It might conceivably have been a spirit of resentment or fear, or self-pity or pride, and it is not unreasonable to suppose, nor is it without supporting evidence, and the opinion of at least a few eminent physicians, that this sort of non-physical condition could be one of the multiple causes of disease. Indeed it appears that it could be such a determining factor in the cause of some diseases that its removal could lead to a rapid recovery of health. It would not be fair, however, to attribute this woman's unhappy condition to her own fault. She was not the only one in the community who suffered from "evil spirits". As the Epistle to the Ephesians says, we all have to fight "against cosmic powers, against the authorities and potentates of this dark (negative) world, against the superhuman forces of evil in the heavens." Such powers are very real and very potent in modern as in ancient society, though we would probably call them by other names. Perhaps they are best understood in terms of what Jung called the "collective unconscious".

It would appear that the woman had come to worship with no thought of being healed, but our Lord in His loving compassion could not bear to leave her as she was. First He spoke to her declaring that she was released from her infirmity. Authoritative utterance is frequently the prelude to healing (Mark i. 27; Luke iv. 36).

In addition to the commanding word by which alone He often healed the sick (Luke iv. 39; v. 24; vi. 10), Jesus also laid His hands on the woman as in Luke iv. 40; v. 13. The cure was instantaneous. That was because there was no resistance in Jesus to the will of God, to which He could therefore give immediate effect by His perfect realisation of the divine presence and power.

The laying on of hands (when it has no special medical or priestly significance) is a simple and natural gesture expressing at the same time both concern and assurance. With or without words it is one way of prayer. When no speech would be appropriate the touch of the hand can say what no words could.

As a means of conveying some comforting or healing power the laying on of hands is usually the accompaniment of a brief spoken prayer or blessing in which the Christian name of the recipient is used. It is thus an emphatic and concentrated form of prayer for a particular person and often to meet a particular need. When emotional and other conditions are right, when the desire for help is matched by the purity of thought which cannot fail to be a channel of divine grace, when there is no resistance to the will of God an astonishing measure of healing may result. Cases have been reported of instantaneous recovery following this simple treatment.

One explanation offered by doctors is that the body may be partially crippled by a disease such as polio or arthritis, and after some years, though there is no longer any active disease present, the limbs remain impotent from habit or disuse. In such circumstances a sudden shock or a sudden recovery of hope and assurance may enable the invalid to resume his lost powers instantaneously. If more co-operation could be obtained between ministers of religion and ministers of medicine one might see many more spectacular healings of this nature.

We do not know all that Jesus said or did to this woman. The Gospel narrative is condensed' and what a modern reporter might have put into some hundreds of words the evangelist presses into little more than headlines. The fact as recorded is that the suffering woman was able to straighten up for the first time in eighteen years.

Instead of being delighted to see the woman restored to health the ruler of the synagogue protested that the Sabbath law had been broken. This small-minded interpretation of the law of God must seem to us almost incredible until we remember how important the leaders of Judaism regarded the keeping of one day in seven entirely for worship. Infringements of this law could bring spiritual loss to the whole community, as the Ruler of the synagogue realised to his credit. But in his excessive zeal for keeping the day exclusively for God he was in danger of excluding God Himself. We can sympathise with the Ruler of the synagogue, though what he said was hardly fair to the people, who had no intention of coming to be healed on the Sabbath but who, having come to worship, were astonished to witness the entirely unexpected healing of the crippled woman. Worship in the synagogue is usually less formal than in most churches and the special attention given to an ailing woman need have caused no sensation. What vexed the Ruler was that in a place and time devoted to the worship of God something had been done which was merely the service of man. But was it? Or is it not, as Jesus said, to the glory of God that suffering should be relieved and infirmity healed?

Our Lord attributed this crippling illness to Satan, the Adversary of God. In our day, using contemporary jargon, we might call it the power of communal thought that is opposed to divine thought, that baneful influence of perverted faith lingering half consciously in the minds of the thoughtless who, without knowing it, are impeding and thwarting the beneficent thoughts of God. The power of negative feeling that lurks in every neighbourhood, to which many decent people contribute far more than they realise, and which is such an important factor in the making of all tragedy and loss, could very well be described as *Satan*, the power that subtly opposes the will of the Almighty. This is one of the results of that liberty of thought which God insists on giving to man and without which there could be no morality or growth in grace.

Probably the Ruler of the synagogue (like so many good people) attributed disease to the will of God and not to rebellion against Him, and so he did not see in the healing of disease a sign that the Kingdom of God was not far off, but rather an unseemly interruption to worship which could easily have been postponed until the service was over.

This event in the synagogue raises the question whether or not the healing of disease and infirmity ought not to be admitted as part of our ordinary acts of public worship. The healing properties of Holy Communion, as well for the body as the soul, are in some churches recognised today as they are also in some of the ancient liturgies. Today all churches are engaged in revising their orders of service and sacraments, and innovations have recently been allowed even by the most conservative churches in which they would not have been considered right even a few years ago. These changes are to be welcomed as attempts to bring into the corporate worship of the people a heightened sense of reality and to relate the sacraments to the secular affairs of life. There are other and perhaps simpler changes which could be even more effective in restoring the worship of our churches to a more prominent place in the affections of the people. More meditative prayer, a healing silence, or an opportunity given for the laying on of hands in an atmosphere of faith. No one who understands the nature of religion would encourage a credulous craving for miracles, but neither would he discourage an eager and assured expectation of the invasion of our worship by the evident action of God.

XVII

THE WIDOW'S SON

"AFTERWARDS Jesus went to a town called Nain, accompanied by his disciples and a large crowd. As he approached the gate of the town he met a funeral. The dead man was the only son of his widowed mother; and many of the townspeople were there with her. When the Lord saw her his heart went out to her, and he said, 'Weep no more.' With that he stepped forward and laid his hand on the bier; and the bearers halted. Then he spoke: 'Young man, rise up!' The dead man sat up and began to talk; and Jesus gave him back to his mother. Deep awe fell upon them all, and they praised God. 'A great prophet has arisen among us', they said, and again, 'God has shown his care for his people.' The story of what he had done ran through all parts of Judaea and the whole neighbourhood." Luke vii. 11–17.

WE COME to a very interesting case indeed for it is one of restoration to health not from sickness but from death. This is a stumbling block to many readers who, though they are ready to believe that the power of our Lord to heal disease was not less wonderful than that of modern medicine, find it hard in all honesty to accept as fact the recovery to life of a person who was actually dead.

Scruples of this kind are to be respected. We must never pretend to believe, or even try to believe, what in our hearts we think incredible. No belief, however edifying, can be of any value to religion unless it is true. Before, however, this miracle is rejected as improbable, some observations may be made.

99

The difference between life and death cannot always be so clearly defined as is supposed. Doctors have declared that after all signs of life have ceased an appreciable time elapses before death occurs. Writers familiar with occult practices in the East have described how living creatures are deprived of life by the power of thought alone. But if the negative act of killing can be done by the concentration of intense corporate thought is it incredible that the positive and beneficent act of restoration to life could be accomplished by the creative thought of a God-filled mind?

Stories are now told of hospital patients who while undergoing treatment collapse and, if news reports are to be believed, actually "die". But by the amazing devices of modern medical skill they are brought back to life and make a good recovery. The period during which patients can remain "dead" is usually a very short time, though in one instance we are told it lasted for 86 minutes. The report laid emphasis on the fact that breathing had actually stopped and that all other signs of life had also ceased.

Now the interesting thing about this modern story is not the alleged facts which it discloses but its effect upon those who heard it. Newspaper reporters one and all expressed admiration for the astonishing powers of medical science. Not one of them had any difficulty in believing that what they had been told was entirely true nor were any sceptical comments recorded on the part of their readers. When people are told that science can raise the dead they are moved to profound wonder at the age in which we live. When they are told that the power of God can raise the dead they smile indulgently!

The questions are (and until we can answer them we had better speak with caution about what can and what cannot be true): Can the divine creative Spirit, acting in and through human minds, exercise transforming and restorative power? and, if it can, Is it unreasonable to suppose that this power could be beyond the normal experience of those who have made no research in this field of knowledge, and who have never tried to use their minds as instruments of a divine purpose? If God does not exist and if, contrary to the Gospel it is the material universe that gives life and the spirit avails nothing (John vi. 63), then the miracles of the New Testament along with all other indications of supernatural power are nothing more than fiction and phantasy. But if, as the psalmist said, man did not make himself but was made by a Creator Spirit, then, if we do not want to lose touch with reality, we shall have to take a closer look at life than materialism has yet dared to do.

The evangelist undoubtedly believed, and intended his readers to believe, that this young man was dead. It may have been a case of premature burial which is still common in the East and may have been even more prevalent in ancient times. But our Lord did not say, as He did in the case of the daughter of Jairus, that the supposedly dead person was only asleep.

If this is a factual story intended to be understood literally how can we account for such an astounding piece of evidence for the Gospel being found in Luke alone, with no parallel in any of the other Gospels? A very pertinent question! We can only reply with another: how does there come to be so much material of the highest devotional value in Luke only, apparently unknown or neglected by the other evangelists?[1]

Our Lord did not think it incredible that God should raise the dead but claimed it as one of the signs that the reign of God had come (Matt. xi. 5). We must beware of setting limits in our own minds to the power of God. There are devout people who believe that God converts but not that He heals. Some believe that He never fails to punish but cannot believe that He never fails to forgive. The author of a popular book on the Christian

[1] Nain is not mentioned elsewhere in Scripture but it has been identified with a small village, now largely in ruins, not far from the place called, in II Kings iv, Shunen, where another widow's son was raised from death by the prophet Elisha (2 Kings iv).

faith adduces as a part of his testimony to Christ the power of prayer to heal diseases. Then in a burst of candour he adds, "Of course I am not talking about fatal diseases such as cancer." Are we justified in putting limits to the power of the Creator of all?

We can look back into antiquity and find evidence of astonishing feats of engineering in a pre-scientific age. How were the enormous blocks of stone which are all that is left to-day of the pre-historic temple at Stonehenge transported from their native quarry and erected on their present site? Some master mind must have contrived to use a degree of physical force almost incredible in a primitive community. There are other unsolved problems of transportation and construction, including the pyramids of Egypt, which can only be classed as wonders of the world. Some day perhaps we shall be able to explain how such things were done and we may yet know more about the power which even in a pre-scientific era was known and used by Jesus and imparted to His disciples to heal the sick and to raise to life some who were accounted dead. As Harold Anson said many years ago: "He (Jesus) came to show us not what God could do and man could not do, but what Man could do, and is intended to do, when he lives the life that God designed for him, and exercises those powers which God places at his disposal."[1]

[1] In *Concerning Prayer* (Macmillan 1918) in chapter on "Prayer and Bodily Health".

XVIII

THE TEN LEPERS

"In the course of his journey to Jerusalem he was travelling through the borderlands of Samaria and Galilee. As he was entering a village he was met by ten men with leprosy. They stood some way off and called out to him, 'Jesus, Master, take pity on us.' When he saw them he said, 'Go and show yourselves to the priests'; and while they were on their way, they were made clean. One of them, finding himself cured, turned back praising God aloud. And he was a Samaritan. At this Jesus said: 'Were not all ten cleansed? The other nine, where are they? Could none be found to come back and give praise to God except this foreigner?' And he said to the man, 'Stand up and go on your way; your faith has cured you.'" Luke xvii. 11–19.

Also read: Leviticus xiii. 45–47, Numbers v. 2–4.

O N HIS WAY to Jerusalem our Lord crossed the border between Galilee and Samaria, or perhaps we should translate verse 11, "Passed along between Samaria and Galilee." This would indicate that Jesus was following the usual route taken by Jews going from Galilee to Jerusalem, which avoided Samaritan territory by going through Perea on the other side of the Jordan.

The frontier between the two countries was a likely place in which to meet a band of lepers, some of them Jews and some of them (or at least one) Samaritan. Their common misery and expulsion from the rest of the community had broken down the racial and religious barriers between them. Standing at a distance, as the law required them to do, they shouted to Jesus and appealed for His help.

Leprosy in the Bible is a name used for a number of skin diseases not all of them accounted fatal. So the men who now accosted Jesus may have had reasonable hope of recovery. What they expected the Lord to do for them is not clear. Perhaps they were only begging, or perhaps they had heard of our Lord's healing power and even of the healing of the leper recorded in Luke v. 12–16. Probably a good deal more conversation took place between Jesus and the lepers than is recorded, but the outcome of it was that Jesus sent them to report to the public authorities who were the priests (Lev. xiv). The Samaritan would go to his own priest. This was an act of faith on the part of the lepers for there could be no object in going to the priests unless they could produce evidence that they were cured.

They had not gone far apparently before they realised that their foul disease had vanished. One of them, the Samaritan, immediately turned back and, with loud praise to God, prostrated himself before Jesus in thanksgiving. He was the only one that came back.

All the others presumably, when they saw that they were healed, rushed on to the priests to be examined and certified as clean. The proceedings took some time and indeed it was only after eight days that a leper could be finally pronounced free from pollution. Perhaps they did think gratefully of Jesus but He was a traveller on the road and how could they overtake Him now? Before we condemn them we had better consider what we should have done in their place.

We cannot suppose that our Lord was grieved by a failure in courtesy on the part of men who must have been naturally excited by their sudden release from a dreadful affliction. What He did observe was a profound difference between two kinds of people. The first are self-conscious in the sense of being very aware of themselves and of their own condition. The second are God-conscious and are aware of the presence and activity of God. Thanksgiving is usually a sign of God-consciousness and its absence the sign of self-consciousness. We give thanks to the glory of God and not primarily for our own good; but, incidentally, genuine praise of God has great therapeutic value. To be absorbed in ourselves is a dangerous as well as an unhappy condition. Thanksgiving lifts our attention from ourselves, if only for a moment, and in so doing releases us from the anxious care and selfish fears which if unchecked could do us much harm.

As prayer should never end without thanksgiving so no experience of recovery from illness, or escape from danger or trouble, should be allowed to pass without a deliberate act of praise to God. Praise is the recognition of the divine power to which we owe our deliverance. To withhold this recognition is to diminish its power for our own good and to reduce our faculty for helping others.

Thanksgiving has the effect of cleansing our minds consciously and unconsciously from the lingering thought of trouble and sickness; without this act of devotion our prayers for healing are not complete. Notice that our Lord again attributed the cure to the faith of the man who was healed.

XIX

SIMON'S WIFE'S MOTHER

"ON leaving the synagogue they went straight to the house of
Simon and Andrew; and James and John went with them. Simon's
mother-in-law was ill in bed with fever. They told him about her at
once. He came forward, took her by the hand, and helped her to her
feet. The fever left her and she waited upon them.

"That evening after sunset they brought to him all who were ill or
possessed by devils; and the whole town was there, gathered at the
door. He healed many who suffered from various diseases, and drove
out many devils. He would not let the devils speak, because they
knew who he was." Mark i. 29–34.

Also read: Matthew viii. 14–17, Luke iv. 38–41.

THIS IS such a simple homely domestic incident that it
could be overlooked. There is nothing spectacular here.
Peter's home was in Capernaum and naturally after the events in
the synagogue, where an insane man was restored to his right
mind by our Lord's authoritative word of command, he took
Jesus home, together with his brother Andrew, and James and
John the sons of Zebedee, whom they must have known as
fishermen on the Lake of Galilee.

On entering the house they found Peter's mother-in-law in
bed with fever. Luke the physician says it was a "great" fever
which must mean that according to the medical classification of
the time it was a very serious one, like a bout of malaria, and not
merely a rise in temperature brought on by excitement or fatigue.

As soon as Jesus had been told of her illness He went to the sick woman and taking her by the hand He helped her to rise. The fever receded and she was able to get up and help entertain the guests.

Could it really have happened so quickly? Is there perhaps an element of oriental enthusiasm and exaggeration that, as some commentators aver, has crept into the Gospel narrative here as elsewhere? Even today in the modern Western world we are often tempted to exaggerate the evidence for divine healing. There must have been people in the ancient world too on whose tongues a story was enhanced by every telling of it. But why should we suspect Mark's simple and straightforward account of what happened? Isn't it because we begin to read the Gospel with a bias towards the materialism of our own age? Such things, we believe, just do not happen! With our scientific education how can we honestly believe that they ever did?

Let us suppose that the incident could be transferred in time and place to our own country and our own age. A young man brings home a party of friends, among them a doctor whose remarkable work has won him a widespread reputation as a physician. On entering they discover that the lady of the house is unwell and has had to lie down in a feverish condition. Of course the host confides in his friend who without hesitation goes to the bedside, takes the patient's pulse, quickly observes the all too obvious symptoms of a high temperature, administers a tablet, holds her hand while the drug takes effect and then helps her up. Her temperature has subsided. She feels fresh and well, whether by the administration of the medicine or the irresistible personality of the doctor or perhaps by both. In a little while she has quite recovered and without further ado is able to assist in the housework.

This is a quite credible story is it not? But why? Because we choose to believe in the efficacy of a drug though not in the power of God! We worship and serve the creature more than the Creator! (Rom. i. 25). We have all experienced feverish headaches, either in ourselves or the members of our families, which have yielded rapidly to our favourite medicines. We should not think it much of a miracle if one moment, or at least one hour, we were on the brink of collapse and completely recovered the next. Mark is fond of the word translated *immediately* but as he uses it perhaps it is the equivalent of the French *alors* without any intention of instantaneous sequence. But there is no need to postulate a long lapse of time. We have known doctors who could restore a completely incapacitated man by the sheer force of personality or confidence or suggestion, or however it might be described by the psychologists, in a remarkably short time. And is it impossible that Jesus of Nazareth, who (whatever else we say about Him) was no ordinary man, restored the sick to health by the exercise of powers that were divine?

What is ridiculous is that we should accord a ready and uncritical belief to the power of drugs or psychology and refuse it to the power of Christ! Many who read the Gospels with great reservations are carried away in ecstatic credulity by every commercial advertisement they see.

That day was the Sabbath and at an earlier hour Jesus had been with His four companions to worship in the synagogue (see Chapter v). At sunset, which marked the end of the Sabbath, people came from all over the town bringing invalids to be healed. They must have had some ground for believing that the man from Nazareth could work wonders. Mark says that all the town came and Jesus healed many. Matthew improves on Mark's original report by reversing the *all* and the *many*. Many came, he says, and He healed them all. At any rate a wide variety of diseases was dealt with. The power that our Lord exercised was not limited to certain *kinds* of illness. Perhaps He healed not so much the disease as the sufferer, so restoring the person to a right relation to life that he became integrated into his total environment or, as the Gospels say, he was *made whole*.

In verse 34 a curious comment is made, repeated in other contexts, to the effect that insane or possessed people hailed Jesus as the Messiah, not knowing of course what they were saying but uttering the uninhibited perceptions of their unconscious minds. Jesus silenced them, says the evangelist, because (at this stage of His ministry at least) He wished to conceal His identity.

There could be a simpler explanation. Of course Jesus did not desire the senseless flattery of the sick-minded even if their adulations did express the unconscious mind of the populace. It is very doubtful, however, if the plaudits of the possessed amounted to a recognition of Jesus as Messiah, a conception which in itself was subject to a wide variety of interpretation. For Jesus to claim divinity for Himself at any stage of His ministry would be quite out of character, though undoubtedly He felt and acknowledged throughout the whole of His public life a strong sense of divine vocation, and a unity with God which He claimed in some degree for all believers. There is no trace in the synoptic Gospels of the rapturous adoration of Jesus which is a feature of the Epistles and reflects the faith of the post-Resurrection Church. There is, however, a factual record of the contemporary belief that He exercised an extraordinary gift of healing.

XX

THE FOURTH GOSPEL

IN THE FOURTH Gospel there are not so many miracles of
healing as in the synoptics and the few there are have received
a quite different kind of treatment. Instead of being briefly
reported as instances of healing, they are rather made the introduction to discourses of some length and are offered as indications or "signs" of the power and purpose of God in sending
His Son Jesus into the world. It would appear that historical
interest yields to religious interest, and that the author is
concerned not so much to preserve incidents in the life of Jesus
as to illustrate the eternal truths which his Gospel is written to
set forth. This could be said of the synoptic Gospels too, but
not nearly to the same extent. All the evangelists are more
interested in religion than in history and use the latter to witness
to the former. But this is far more true of John than of the other
Gospels, and the question arises, are we to understand the
miracles in John as factual and historical, or as symbolic and
mystical?

In attempting to answer this question we must keep two
considerations in mind – (1) It is not a new question but goes
as far back as the early fathers. The fourth Gospel has all down
the ages won the hearts of simple readers who found in it no
problem at all but only a profundity of truth expressed in
language they could understand at the deepest level, and
concerned with realities which they recognised to be the stuff of
life. It would be difficult today to say anything of value about

this Gospel which has not been said already. We can only give thanks for a book which has been recognised in all ages, and even beyond the bounds of Christian faith, as one of the highest religious value.

(2) While in John historical interest seems to be secondary to devotional interest, it would be quite wrong to say that John is indifferent to history. He clearly corrects the synoptic narrative not only in a number of details but also in some matters of major importance. John, who mentions the last supper only incidentally to the feet washing in the upper room, records the date as the night before the Passover and not, as the synoptics have it, on the Passover itself. Many scholars now agree that on this important question of chronology John must be right. Not such widespread agreement has been won for John's placing of the "Cleansing of the Temple" near the beginning of our Lord's public ministry instead of at the end, where the synoptics make it a contributing cause of the arrest and trial of Jesus. Throughout the book there is evidence of an intimate knowledge of the geography of Palestine and of the language and customs of the country.

So when we come to study the healing miracles in John we must not too rashly conclude that they are examples of religious fiction told only for their moral value. It is more likely that they are based on recollections of actual happenings which the evangelist uses to illustrate the religious truths which are his main concern.

The authorship of the fourth gospel has always been a problem to students of the New Testament. It is possible that the John, whose name is attached to the book, was the son of Zebedee and the apostle who in the *Acts of the Apostles* is associated with Peter in the early days of the Church. This assumption, however, has been questioned from very early times, and apart from the desire to claim for this gospel apostolic authorship there is little to be said historically in its favour.

Eusebius, the ancient Church historian, tells us that besides the Apostle there was another John known as the *Elder* or *Presbyter* also associated with Ephesus. It may be that this other John was the author of the Gospel.

Before passing on to consider the miracles that John records it may be worth while to pause a moment to reflect that in this Gospel healing is something more than a cure. It is a kind of conversion. The change of body is also a change of heart. Something of religious significance happens when a sick man becomes a healthy man. It is not a successful experiment in chemistry or an achievement of the new psychology; it is something which God had done before which, to those who have the eyes to see it, will stand in reverence, as witnesses of an act of God.

XXI

DO YOU WANT TO BE WELL?

"LATER on Jesus went up to Jerusalem for one of the Jewish festivals. Now at the Sheep-Pool in Jerusalem there is a place with five colonnades. Its name in the language of the Jews is Bethesda. In these colonnades there lay a crowd of sick people, blind, lame, and paralysed. Among them was a man who had been crippled for thirty-eight years. When Jesus saw him lying there and was aware that he had been ill a long time, he asked him, 'Do you want to recover?' 'Sir,' he replied, 'I have no one to put me in the pool when the water is disturbed, but while I am moving, someone else is in the pool before me.' Jesus answered, 'Rise to your feet, take up your bed and walk.' The man recovered instantly, took up his stretcher, and began to walk." John v. 1–9.

THE INCIDENT recorded in Chapter iv. 43–54 is so like that of Matthew viii. 5–11 and Luke vii. 2–10 that it may be taken as another version of the healing of the Centurion's boy. The official whose boy (either son or servant) is dying is probably the same who won the admiration of our Lord by his reasoned faith in the authority of Universal Mind to order all things in accordance with his own perfect will. John, however, introduces a remark of Jesus which, though the question seems out of place in this context, is important, "Will you never believe without seeing signs and portents?" A faith that is fed on miracle is not healthy. If we believe only because we are forced out of our better judgment by stunning prodigies, our belief is not based on any balanced and stable conviction. The reason for the insertion of this saying of our Lord just here is to contrast idle curiosity and the desire to see a show, with the genuine cry of human need to divine power.

Does this mean that the healing miracles are *not* signs and wonders? How are we to distinguish between the healing acts of our Lord which He Himself said were signs of God's controlling power and the sort of sensational exhibition which is here deplored? Perhaps the difference could be put like this: there is a public interest in what are announced as miracles of healing which seeks not so much the glory of God in the release of man from the bondage of disease and infirmity, as the satisfaction felt in a good story.

It would not be true to draw too close a comparison between the work of Christ and that of the Health Services but the healing miracles have on the whole just as much in common with the dedicated and compassionate work of the medical professions as with some of those demonstrations of healing that are given at public meetings. Jesus healed,[1] apparently with as little publicity as He could, for the good of humanity and the glory of God (two things which are never opposed to each other) but not with any other motive such as the advancement of His cause or the increase of His popularity.

We pass on to the case of the man who had been lying at the Pool of Bethzatha for thirty-eight years waiting to be healed. A variant reading to Bethzatha (House of Figs) is the familiar Bethesda (House of Mercy) but the place cannot be identified in modern Jerusalem. Verse 4 and the last words of verse 3 in the Authorised Version are an explanatory interpolation and are usually omitted.

The special interest of this story is the question which Jesus put to the waiting invalid, *Do you want to be well?* The man, if he had not been so patient, might have replied, "What do you think I'm doing here? Thirty-eight years I've been waiting just

---

[1] Matthew xi. 2–6; Mark i. 37–8, 44, ii. 12, v. 43, vii. 36, viii. 26.

for the chance of a cure — thirty-eight years, and he says, Do you want to be well? I ask you!"

It does seem rather a tactless question to ask of one who was so obviously waiting to be cured and who for so long had never given up hope. "Just give me half a chance," he might have said, "but that's what I've never had. With all this pushing and scrambling what chance have I with my infirmity to get into the water first, and no one to help me! It's not fair! But that's life. That's just what happens — those that need most get least. Thirty-eight years! Is there any one of them who deserves to be healed more than I? But me, nobody cares enough to help me! I'm surrounded by all this mob, yet I'm alone! Not a real friend in the world. No one I can trust. Do I want to be cured! What do you take me for?"

How true it all was and yet how false. It is not usually our circumstances that are so important but the way in which we confront them. What a pitiful tale this man could tell — all those years of disappointment and frustration! The best part of his life had gone waiting for something that never came. It was not as though it had been his own fault either; he had waited and waited, never giving up hope, but nothing had happened.

But there was another side to all this. All those years he had been growing used to his illness, till now perhaps he could hardly bear to part with it. After more than half a lifetime how could he face the world and all its demands? Life could be very hard. If only he could get a start he was confident he could go on, but he had no one he could trust to help him. He had never heard the modern word *rehabilitation* but he knew what it meant. He knew very well that once he got his health he would have to adjust himself to the harsh necessities of life. Health lays upon us responsibilities which illness can make much easier to bear, if it cannot get rid of them entirely. This man had come to a time of life when he could not escape some survey of his own achievements. They had not been impressive.

He never had done much for anyone, an intolerable thought until he remembered that no one had done much for him. He was not to blame. He had never had a chance! Every time an opportunity had offered itself he had failed to take it, not by his own choice but because no one had helped him. He had never done much; he had never been much; no one regretted it more than he did himself. But he had an excellent excuse; he was ill.

And here was One asking him, Do you want to get rid of your excuse for failure? Are you willing to face life without the crutches of infirmity? Do you really *want* to be well? We can imagine that the conversation the man had with Jesus was much longer than is recorded here. This was the gist perhaps of the plea that our Lord made to him in what may have been an hour or more of very friendly but frank talk. If the sick man expected sympathy he must have been surprised, if disappointed, at the Lord's attitude. Here was One who did not offer sympathy, One who could afford not to offer it. He gave not sympathy but help, very practical help. But first He had to explain that healing lay not in the pool, nor in the agitation of the water, nor in the race to get there first but in the deep beliefs of the sick man's heart. There were a hundred ways that God could use to heal him if he believed it possible and really desired to take what God willed him to have.

How long, we might wonder, did it take this sufferer to realise that God was willing to do far more for him than he was willing to accept from God? His limitations were imposed upon him not by God but by himself. God was able to take him out into a larger life if only he were willing. As he listened to Jesus he began to see healing in a new light. It was a condition not of the body only but also of the mind and indeed of the whole person. Health was something that required decision, courage, trust. He was no longer going to wait for angelic agitations in his circumstances, nor for kindhearted neighbours to push him in the right direction, but then and there he would surrender

his sense of grievance and self-pity and in the name of God
walk!

We can be sure that our Lord put His question to the invalid
gently with no touch of censure or contempt. His purpose as
ever was not to condemn but to save. Yet it is a question that
has to be asked, perhaps with some insistence, not of other
people but of ourselves. Do we *want* to throw off our limitations?
Granted that growth in grace is a slow process, do we really
wish to be other than we are, or have we grown so used to ourselves that any change of character would frighten us? Leave
aside for the moment the question of what God can and will do
for us, and put it to yourself, do I want to be from now on
perfectly fit, without the least excuse for failure or evasion of
responsibility to the end of my life? Do I *want* the abundant
life, and the joy unspeakable, and the power that worketh
mightily within me? Do I desire above all else to be fit for the
conflict with pretence and snobbery and greed, to fight the *good*
fight without malingering? If God were willing to use me on a
delicate and dangerous mission would I be ready to go?

When we receive absolution in church (or wherever else God
gives it) we receive *release*. It is the power of God to set us free
from all that weighs us down and shuts us up within our own
small measurements of life. It is His gift to comprehend with all
the saints what is the length and breadth, the height and depth
of life and to know the love of Christ. What God wants us to
have is liberty and enlargement; from the obvious dangers of
both it is not surprising we shrink. There can be little doubt that
God's will for us is far beyond our own. We need not be like
the man of whom his doctor said, "He is not in bed because he
is ill, he is ill because he's in bed"! It could be that lying on a
mat is safer on the whole than taking it up to walk.

Of course it must not be suggested that this man was not
really ill after all but only thought he was, still less that he was
feigning sickness to escape contact with real life. We may not

go beyond the Scripture record from which we see that one who had been laid aside for thirty-eight years did, after encountering Christ, declare his readiness to step out into fullness of life. As soon as he was willing he found that God was too. There was no need to wait for the troubling of the waters, nor for anybody else to help him. He picked up his bed and walked out into the world.

The process of healing often begins with a decision. The abundant life is offered to us all, but we must make up our minds to accept it. It is the nature of God to offer, but never to impose. He sets before us an alternative but does not dictate our choice. His call to us is always to change our minds, but He will never change them for us nor, like some foolish parents who make all the decisions for their children, take from us the responsibility of freedom. Few people retain health by chance. It is by a conscious and deliberate choice that we receive the gifts of God.

XXII

ONE THING I KNOW

"As he went on his way Jesus saw a man blind from his birth. His disciples put the question, 'Rabbi, who sinned, this man or his parents? Why was he born blind?' 'It is not that this man or his parents sinned,' Jesus answered; 'he was born blind that God's power might be displayed in curing him. While daylight lasts we must carry on the work of him who sent me; night comes, when no one can work. While I am in the world I am the light of the world.'

"With these words he spat on the ground and made a paste with the spittle; he spread it on the man's eyes, and said to him, 'Go and wash in the pool of Siloan.' (The name means 'sent'.) The man went away and washed, and when he returned he could see." John ix. 1–7.

Also read rest of chapter.

THIS IS ANOTHER instance of healing in which recovery took some time and was the result of treatment by methods which were well known and much in use at the time. The evangelist makes it clear that a cure of this kind could be a miracle to the glory of God.

This narrative asks and answers some very interesting questions which still concern many people today. (1) Why had God allowed this man to be born blind? Jewish faith reverently attributed all disease not to God but to man's disobedience to God. Suffering, they saw clearly, was the consequence of sin, or rebellion against God, and not the will of God Himself. In this surely they were partly right. But could it be asserted that infirmity and disease in little children was the result of their sin, or could children inherit the suffering due to their parents' sin?

Before we revolt from this thought as abhorrent to all belief in the goodness and love of God we must recognise the question as one that demands a better answer than is usually given it even in our own day. We will not of course attribute sickness, whether in children or adults, as punishment inflicted by God. That sickness is largely the consequence of ungodly thoughts and negative emotions and in that sense may be regarded as one result of estrangement from God (though not necessarily on the part of the sufferer) is a much more credible doctrine than any which would see it as a manifestation of divine wrath or justice. That is to say disease is not sent by God but is part of the evil that humanity brings upon itself by its rejection of God's will and neglect of His law.

This does not mean that we can necessarily trace sickness or any other adversity to the personal sin of the sufferer. Our Lord's answer to the disciples' question is perfectly clear. The blindness was caused neither by the man's own fault nor that of his parents. The suggestion that the sick are suffering the due reward of their sins could be as false as it is cruel. There are cases, indeed, in which the sufferer has contributed to the cause of his illness and helped to bring it upon himself. We are seldom in trouble without having done something to attract it to ourselves. But to say that all sickness is our own personal fault would be a sweeping statement unsupported by evidence.

And yet there is just here an unpopular truth that should not be overlooked. Sickness or any other trouble is in one sense brought upon us by our own fault. If we were rightly adjusted to our total environment would not everything be well with us? With regard to other people we must speak with caution and compassion, but with regard to our own troubles we may find that in large measure their continuance is caused by some spiritual deficiency in our own character. When we become the victims of accident or illness we naturally demand to know how it happened, what was the cause of the trouble. There will always be found circumstances which can be blamed for it, but it may be that the chief causal factor, without which we would have remained immune from the misfortune which overtook us, lies in ourselves. There is evidence to indicate that a large percentage of all accidents are not merely accidental but partly caused by the emotional or mental condition of the persons involved. This is true also in the case of illness. There is something within ourselves as well as something without that makes us succumb to the trouble. "The fault, dear Brutus, lies not in our stars but in ourselves," and though systems of philosophy which are calculated to relieve us of responsibility for our condition are always popular, the true Gospel places the blame firmly on us.

This is all so contrary to prevailing opinion at the present time that it will be received undoubtedly with great reserve. Yet it ought to be a relief to know that our troubles could be largely overcome by some change not so much in our circumstances as in ourselves. If I am the helpless victim of forces outside of my control I am in a very unhappy condition indeed. But if some change in myself can deliver me from my sufferings then the key to the dungeon lies in my own heart, and the way to health and salvation is not far to seek. Perhaps the real trouble is that most of us do not want to change. Transformation of character is too great a price to pay for that highest welfare for which God made us. It is easier for us to go on as we are and to put up with our afflictions. So our answer to the question in Chapter xxi., Do you want to be well? becomes a reluctant but habitual NO.

What then are we to make of disease? Jesus was not so concerned about how it came as about how it must go. The only purpose of God with regard to illness is to get rid of it, and so the answer to the question, Why did this affliction fall upon this man? is *To manifest God's healing power*. This is *not* to say that God makes people ill so that He can display His power in restoring them to health. The disciples were virtually asking, "What's the good of this blindness – what purpose does it serve?", to which our Lord's reply is "No good at all." The only way in which illness can contribute to the glory of God is by the healing of it.

This is not to deny that many infirmities and afflictions are borne with a saintly courage that is an example to all. Sickness does not in itself make for saintliness, as most nurses know, but we have all known patients who bore their sufferings with a fortitude and courage that spoke of their faith more convincingly than any words. Surely such courage is to the glory of God?

This needs clear thinking. It is not the suffering or the sickness that gives glory to God but the spirit in which it is borne. Many gallant social workers of all kinds give glory to God by the patience, wisdom and kindness by which they help people who are living in conditions which are certainly *not* to the glory of God.

Bad housing, bad health and bad legislation may give opportunity for many virtues and even call out virtues which would not otherwise be seen to such a degree of heroism; but this does not sanctify the unholy conditions of living which provide the occasion of the heroism. There are many sufferers for whom we have the highest admiration. The courage with which they bear their infirmities gives glory to God but the infirmities themselves do not claim our admiration in the least degree. Rather we would do all we could to abolish them. We give thanks for all those who labour to alleviate such suffering and to find the way by which society can be delivered from it for all time.

As the story is continued in the remainder of the chapter interest shifts from the relief of a physical blindness to the power of one who can heal the spiritually blind. The moral is that he is the servant of God who can actually do the work of God. In what sense can a man be God's servant? Not by sitting in an office or enjoying a reputation, but by putting the will of God into action in works of compassion. Above all the servant of God is one who can enlighten men, healing them of their moral blindness. What is it after all, John would ask, that makes Jesus our Saviour? Not the fact of His divine appointment, though that is not in question, but the fact that He actually and factually enables men to see. Those who can say of Jesus, "I may not know the correct theology in which to describe Him, but one thing I do know, whereas life was for me a fog, now I can see where I am going," have a better claim to be Christians than some whose professions are very correct but not so relevant to life.

The over-cautious attitude of the religious authorities to the Church's ministry of healing follows in this incident a familiar pattern. It is declared (1) that claims have been made which cannot be substantiated; or (2) even if they can, the healing has been done at the wrong time and in the wrong way; and (3) that the agency of healing is unknown and therefore untrustworthy; (4) that only God can heal (which is exactly what the Church's ministry is saying) and that He does it only through the regular channels. The vital question is, Can grace be imparted otherwise than through the official pipe-lines, medical or ecclesiastical? Those who answer this question in the affirmative are still in danger of being put out of the synagogue. Read the whole chapter again and see what it means.

XXIII

THE STRANGE CASE OF LAZARUS

Read John xi. 1-46

WE COME NOW to what is perhaps the most problematic of all the miracles of healing in the Gospels, the raising of Lazarus from the dead. Several very sincere Christian scholars have believed that this chapter, like others in John, is not concerned with historical fact so much as with doctrine, and that the story has been preserved for its devotional value, not for any factual contribution it can make to the Gospel narrative.

There is much to say for this view. Apart from the question whether or not the story is inherently credible, or relates an event which could not possibly have happened, the whole chapter is full of religious teaching of which the raising of Lazarus is the illustration. There are many meaningful sentences here which have slipped naturally into the devotional life of all Christians. "I know that whatsoever thou wilt ask of God, God will give thee." "The Master is here and calls for you." "Jesus wept." "Said I not unto thee that if thou wouldest believe, thou shouldest see the glory of God." "Father I thank Thee that Thou hast heard me, and I know that Thou hearest me always." But above all the familiar words, "I am the Resurrection and the life: he that believeth in me, though he were dead, yet shall he live: and whosoever believeth in me shall never die." Was it not for the sake of such abiding truths as these that St. John wrote this chapter rather than to record an incident which, taken literally, could be considered to diminish rather than increase its religious significance?

It could be said with some truth that the sharp distinction which the modern world makes between parable and actual fact was hardly recognised in antiquity and certainly not in much of holy scripture. What we call the "historical" books were described as "prophecies", meaning that which is said or written for the edification of the readers. Our Lord's own teaching was largely given through the medium of similitude or parable (Matt. xiii. 34; Mark iv. 33–34) and no intelligent student of the Gospels would insist that the parables must be based (though probably some of them were) on fact. John does not record the parables of Jesus, as the other evangelists had done, but he puts his own recollections of the Lord's teaching in parabolic form. That the greater part of Chapter xi. is to be understood as teaching by analogy, and truth expressed in the form of story based only partially on fact, is therefore a suggestion that is worth consideration.

The most formidable argument, however, against the historicity of the raising of Lazarus is not the nature of the narrative, but the fact of its entire omission from the other Gospels. How could such an astounding miracle as the restoration to life of a man who had been dead for some days remain unknown to the sources from which the synoptic Gospels were compiled? The fourth Gospel, it must be remembered, was probably compiled towards the end of the first century, fifty or sixty years after the events it records, while Mark may have been compiled between 60 and 70 A.D., probably from documents and traditions that were perhaps a decade or two earlier. Is it conceivable that a miracle of this magnitude, one that, we are told, had such widespread repercussions as to provide one of the motives for the determination of the Jewish authorities to prosecute Jesus (John xii. 10–11), was not known by the earlier writers, or if known, that it was ignored by them?

This is the argument from silence which is always precarious, though in this case it does seem to have some cogency. Counter questions might be asked such as, How could the ritual in the upper room in which our Lord broke bread and poured out wine to signify His own death, and which was afterwards to become the sacrament of the Lord's Supper, fail to be mentioned in the fourth Gospel? Or how could such fundamental Christian teaching as is to be found for example in the fifteenth chapter of St. Luke be omitted from all the other Gospels? How does any description of the Ascension such as is given by St. Luke come to be absent from the other Gospels? Omission in itself can never be a conclusive argument against authenticity.

Nevertheless it may be felt that the main reason for rejecting this chapter as matter of fact is the inability of modern commentators to believe that such a thing could happen. If we come to this chapter firmly convinced that its contents are impossible no other arguments are necessary to dispose of the event which it records. We are often reminded of the difference between the mentality of the first century Christians and that of our own, and if we are to understand the New Testament aright this must never be forgotten. To read back into the Apostolic Church ideas that belong to the Church of today is an error into which many commentators fall. It is not that the essential Gospel of the Church has changed, but the vehicles of thought, in which it is conveyed to the understanding of the people, vary from generation to generation. In our own age, dominated as it is by the advance of knowledge in the field of natural science, we inevitably and rightly try to express religious truth in terms of what is interesting and meaningful to the contemporary mind. In the first century the evangelists did the same and expressed the central truths of Christian faith in the thought forms of their own time.

In telling the story of the recovery of Lazarus we would be inclined to strip it of all that seems to conflict with modern knowledge. We would be eager to state the facts and to present them in a way that would claim the credence of scientifically minded people. We would tone down the miraculous features of the event, if we could not exclude them altogether, but we would build up the psychological factors in the case, and try to commend our report to the hardheaded, critical, materialistic public of our time. In the ancient world, however, there was no bias in favour of the natural as opposed to the supernatural. In recording an event a touch of the miraculous would be considered helpful in securing for it widespread interest and belief. Some elements that a modern narrator would be inclined to leave out, an ancient writer would be inclined to put in. We may be sure that if we could transport a modern newspaper reporter back to Bethany at the time of Lazarus's death he would bring back essentially the same story, couched in very different language but more credible to modern prejudice.

The greatest difference of all between most modern writers and the authors of the New Testament is that the latter had a frank and firm belief in the supernatural, to which they attributed much that later centuries have attributed solely to the natural. They believed that in all nature, animate and inanimate, there was an invisible power at work, both creative and redemptive, and that no object could either exist or be rightly understood except as the manifestation of this invisible divine energy. We might say that for them supernatural action was entirely natural. We must not suppose that people today are on the whole more intelligent or less gullible than those of the ancient world; it is only that they prefer to be deceived by modern methods.

We can imagine a future century in which historians will look back on this with mild amusement at the materialism which dominated so much of the twentieth century, including that of men of learning and culture. But even more amusing will be the popular superstitions to which many have become a prey even though they have been emancipated from belief in Bible stories as from the fairy tales of the nursery. Students of this age looking back upon us from some generations hence may be refreshed to find that in all the welter of our scientific obscurantism there were still some who were simple enough to believe in miracle, as the manifestation in the natural world of supernatural or divine power.

Let us try to reconstruct the story as John might have told it if he had been writing not for his own time but for ours, and keeping in mind what has already been said in our study of the dead boy at Nain (Ch. XVII). Jesus with His disciples, or some of them, was in retreat, partly for the preparation of the disciples for the events which were to come (and for which even up to the last day of their Master's life they seem to have remained sadly unprepared) and partly for safety from the plots of those who wished to take His life.

The element of personal danger to Jesus during this period is underestimated by most commentators. There are aspects of the triumphal entry to Jerusalem which indicate that though the Church later came to see in this event the fulfilment of a prophecy of Messianic significance, the disciples did not realise what it meant at the time. Perhaps they were absorbed with the problem of how to gain access to the city, as our Lord was determined to do, without being arrested by the forces which must have been on the lookout for Him. The use of a pre-arranged password to obtain the ass on which Jesus rode suggests the need for secrecy; and the mingling of the disciples with the crowd of pilgrims going up to the festival, while the Lord Himself naturally assumed the leadership and became the centre of enthusiasm, was a successful strategy by which the enemies of Christ were outwitted.

In the following days Jesus appeared in public only when surrounded by the crowds of people who loved to listen to Him and in whose presence His enemies dared not interfere (John

vii. 45–49 – also xi. 57). The fact that Jesus and His men left the city after nightfall to encamp on the Mount of Olives may be explained by the overcrowding caused in Jerusalem by the invasion of many hundreds of thousands of pilgrims, or it may have been that there was nowhere in the city safe from those who were searching for them. Jesus was in fact a "wanted man". Secrecy again appears in the finding of the upper room in which the last supper took place and in the end it was only by the treachery of one of His own company that the security of the Garden of Gethsemane was broken.

Jesus had faithful friends, however, who were daring enough to keep in touch with Him secretly and from these He learned that His friend Lazarus at Bethany, the brother of Martha and Mary and a man devoted to His cause, was seriously ill. His first impulse must have been to go to the help of the sick man, but more than His own safety was at stake and He waited for further information. It soon came to tell Him that Lazarus had sunk into unconsciousness. Jesus now determined to go, though Thomas probably voiced the opinion of all the disciples when he declared that a visit to Bethany would prove fatal. This did not prevent them from accompanying Jesus who, on arrival at the village, did not consider it safe to go to the house which He knew so well (which now may have been watched by agents sent to arrest Him) but met Martha outside the village. Martha passed the word secretly to Mary to come and meet Him at the tomb in which the body of Lazarus had been laid. It must be kept in mind that a grave of this kind could be a place of hiding as well as of burial. Notwithstanding Martha's protest the stone which closed the cave-like sepulchre was removed.

People had now gathered round and Jesus, looking up from the darkness of the sepulchre to the light of heaven, prayed to God in thanksgiving. He was so sure of the power of God, and of the efficacy of prayer that He gave thanks in advance for what was going to happen. Then He called aloud to Lazarus by name. The narrative records no other treatment than that of the spoken word (and perhaps of days of prayer that had gone before) though we cannot be sure that everything that our Lord did was carefully observed. Then, as one who had been awaiting a call, the entombed man came out, still wrapped in his grave clothes. The crowd that by now had grown, eager to see the man who had been dead, probably prevented our Lord's arrest for that time, but the spies among them duly reported back to the authorities. There was every motive to hush up the event, significant as it was, for security reasons, and thus an important miracle of healing was left out of the main stream of Gospel tradition.

XXIV

WALKING, LEAPING AND PRAISING GOD

"ONE day at three in the afternoon, the hour of prayer, Peter and
John were on their way up to the temple. Now a man who had been
a cripple from birth used to be carried there and laid every day by
the gate of the temple called 'Beautiful Gate', to beg from people as
they went in. When he saw Peter and John on their way into the
temple he asked for charity. But Peter fixed his eyes on him, as
John did also, and said, 'Look at us.' Expecting a gift from them,
the man was all attention. And Peter said, 'I have no silver or gold;
but what I have I give you: in the name of Jesus Christ of Nazareth,
walk.' Then he grasped him by the right hand and pulled him up;
and at once his feet and ankles grew strong; he sprang up, stood on
his feet, and started to walk. He entered the temple, leaping and
praising God as he went. Everyone saw him walking and praising
God, and when they recognized him as the man who used to sit
begging at Beautiful Gate, they were filled with wonder and amazement at what had happened to him." Acts iii. 1–10.

THE HEALING MINISTRY of Christ did not come to an end
with the death of Jesus, but remained as part of the witness
of the early Church. One triumphant feature of the Resurrection
was that the healing power of the Lord persisted in the faith
and practice of the Apostles. Just as our Lord had gone about
healing all that were sick in His Galilean ministry, now after
His crucifixion the power of the living Christ was still at work.

Philip, Stephen and Paul are all said to have practised
healing, which seems to have been a recognised part of the
Church's ministry. It is noteworthy that the opponents of the
Church, like the critics of Jesus, are never said to deny the fact

of healing but only to protest that the healing has been done in the wrong way or in the wrong place. Modern condemnation of unorthodox healing is usually based on the belief that it is illusory or temporary and thus gives rise to false hopes which can be cruelly disappointed later. There is no objection made about healing in the New Testament where the wonderful cures accomplished by Jesus and His disciples are never doubted though sometimes attributed to undesirable sources of power.

Of all the healing miracles recorded in the *Acts* we must be content to pick out one – the restoration to active life of the cripple at the Gate Beautiful, one of the entrances to the Temple at Jerusalem. The event described here has some resemblance to that at Bethesda recorded in the fifth chapter of John. Peter and John were on their way to observe the afternoon hour of prayer when they were accosted by a man who appealed to them for alms. This man was a cripple who was brought daily to the Temple gate to practise his profession. In some eastern countries beggars were a recognised social group and sometimes had the equivalent of a modern Trade Union to represent their interests.

It is always hard to know how to respond to the appeal of a beggar. In Western civilization there should be no beggars as in most countries State aid is provided for all who are in genuine need. Begging both in the West and in the East can be a profession and sometimes a lucrative one, the appearance of misery being part of its recognised equipment. Yet beggars are part of the human family, and we cannot pretend that they are not there nor satisfy our conscience by the reflection that they *ought* not to be there. Neither can a coin tossed towards them be a substitute for Christian brotherhood. It was Henry Drummond who said that we should never give money to beggars, for we owe them so much more. We are all surrounded by many different kinds of needy people. If we really care for them we shall not be content to make them the objects of our charity.

Peter and John knew this and so they did not walk past the beggar, as though he were an embarrassing anachronism which they did not wish to see, but stopped to share with him the fellowship which was another name for the Church. It was as though they said, "Just look at us: are we the kind of men from whom you'd expect largesse! We haven't got it. As far as money goes we're as poor as you are, but we do have something to give you – a faith that works!" Then bidding the man look them in the face, which he was eager to do in expectation of alms, Peter took him by the hand. "In the name of Jesus Christ of Nazareth," he said, "get up and walk," and he pulled him to his feet. To his astonishment the beggar found that he had strength to stand and he followed Peter and John into the Temple, walking and leaping and praising God.

Some who find it hard to believe in the power of mind or spirit or in any kind of energy that cannot be measured and explained, dismiss this cure of a cripple as a pious exaggeration, attributing to the Christian community such miraculous signs of the favour of God as are predicted in the 35th chapter of Isaiah. This is the kind of explanation that is harder to believe than the thing it explains. There are instances in modern Christian practice of such apparently instantaneous recovery, though usually they have been preceded by a prolonged period, sometimes by years, of prayer. There are diseases which when cured leave the patient crippled. The disease which caused the infirmity is no longer active but the patient has acquired the habit of disablement and adjusted himself to it. A sudden authoritative and convincing word of assurance could have the effect of liberating such an invalid from his infirmity. This has happened so often in modern life that it is hard to deny that it could have occurred in the early Church.

We believe in this miracle, however, not because it can be

paralleled in modern medical practice but as an instance of the power of God to govern and control material conditions. That there is a divine intelligence at work to create and redeem and heal is simple basic faith not only for Christianity but also for all religion. If God is ceaselessly active, as the Gospels say He was in Christ, then this healing activity is constantly present waiting only to be put into effective operation by our belief in it, as love must always wait for response before it can take more than tentative action.

It is evident that our Lord had a technique of His own for putting the healing power of God into operation. He called it faith, by which He meant at least the realisation of God as the source of all life and well-being and a simple trust in His goodness. Jesus imparted this technique of healing to the disciples when He sent them out to preach the Gospel and to heal the sick (Luke ix. 1-2; x. 9; Matt. x. 1, 8; Mark iii. 14-15). They had learned the secret of healing and had practised it successfully (Luke x. 17-20) though with some perplexing failures (Mark ix. 14-28). And now it was part of the witness of the incipient Church to the power of the risen Christ.

How we may wish today that the Church had never lost this power to heal. It is sometimes said that the power of Christ to heal has not been lost but continued in the advance of medical science and the compassion for sufferers that has taken hospitals and homes of healing to all parts of the world. This is part of the truth, and we may well be thankful for it. We discern the spirit of Christ not only in medical missions but also in the dedicated skill of doctors and nurses in every land.

Yet how much we have to learn, and how much we are unable to do. Scientific research, like the disciples after the Transfiguration, though it has had many triumphs, can sometimes only stand baffled by failure, as it asks of life — Why? Why could not we cast it out? Why can't we find the cure?

The answer now as then is, It can be done only by prayer, by a new response to life, by a new disposition to believe in God as the controlling Power. The secret is known to those who can change their mentality and believe the good news that the spirit is in command and not the flesh, and that the whole material world is dominated by the inspiration of love and joy and peace. In a faithless generation it is hard for us to realise that the God who hides Himself is nevertheless God, and though He is hid from the wise and erudite He may be seen by childlike minds. As the Epistle says: By faith we see that the universe was formed by the word (or the uttered thought) of God, so that the visible had its origin in the invisible.